BLOCKCHAIN CONSORTIUMS
A COMPREHENSIVE HANDBOOK

I0480013

INDIA · SINGAPORE · MALAYSIA

Notion Press

No.8, 3rd Cross Street
CIT Colony, Mylapore
Chennai, Tamil Nadu – 600004

First Published by Notion Press 2020
Copyright © Varun Singhi, Murthy Chitlur, Srinivas Mahankali 2020
All Rights Reserved.

ISBN 978-1-64951-762-3

BLOCKCHAIN CONSORTIUMS

A COMPREHENSIVE HANDBOOK

Analyzing the
Business Model of the future

Varun Singhi Murthy Chitlur
Srinivas Mahankali

INDIA · SINGAPORE · MALAYSIA

IND!CACADEMY

INDIC PLEDGE

- *I celebrate our civilisational identity, continuity & legacy in thought, word and deed.*

- *I believe our indigenous thought has solutions for the global challenges of health, happiness, peace and sustainability.*

- *I shall seek to preserve, protect and promote this heritage and in doing so,*
  - *discover, nurture and harness my potential,*
  - *connect, cooperate and collaborate with fellow seekers,*
  - *advance diversity and inclusivity in the society.*

ABOUT INDIC ACADEMY

Indic Academy is a non-traditional 'university' for traditional knowledge. We seek to bring about a global renaissance based on Indic civilizational and indigenous thought. We are pursuing a multidimensional strategy across time, space and cause by establishing centers of excellence, transforming intellectuals and building an ecosystem.

Indic Academy is pleased to support this book.

This book is dedicated to our daughters:

Lisa Singhi

Hitha Chitlur

Deepika Mahankali

And all daughters worldwide

Your feedback is invaluable to us.

If you recently bought this book, we would love to hear from you. You can do this by writing a review on Amazon or the online store from where you purchased this book. As part of our continual service improvement process, we love to hear real client experiences and feedback.

How does it work? To post a review in Amazon, just log in to your account and click on the Create Your Own Review button (under Customer Reviews) of the relevant product page. You can find examples of product reviews in Amazon. If you purchased from another online store, simply follow their procedures.

What happens when I submit my review? Once you have submitted your review, send us an email at bct4nip@gmail.com with the link to your review so we can properly thank you for your feedback.

Contents

Preface *17*

Acknowledgements *19*

About the Authors *21*

Chapter 1.0   Blockchain – The World of Decentralization 25

    1.1   Introduction 25

    1.2   Origin and Definition of Blockchain 26

        1.2.1   Resilient Data Structures of Blockchain 29

    1.3   Applications of Blockchain Technology 39

    1.4   Blockchain's Value Proposition Across
        Industries and Use Cases 39

    1.5   Digital Representation of Assets and
        Rights on a Blockchain Vide Tokenization 46

    1.6   Blockchain – A Key Catalyst for Secured
        Automation and a World of Trusted
        Transactions 48

Chapter 2.0   Blockchain Consortium 55

    2.1   What is Meant by 'Consortium' in General? 55

    2.2   Blockchain Consortium Overview 56

    2.3   Why Consortiums Are Critical for
        Blockchain Technology? 58

2.4   Benefits from Blockchain Consortiums 60

2.5   Roles in Blockchain Consortium 62

Chapter 3.0   Blockchain Consortiums – Different Flavours 65

3.1   Overview of Different Flavours 65

3.2   Blockchain Consortium – Best Fit
Industry Sectors 69

3.3   Blockchain Consortium Business Models 72

Chapter 4.0   Consortium Formation...77

4.1   Overview...77

4.2   Nailing the Pre-consortium Agreement –
Key Considerations 79

    4.2.1   Define the New Entity's Business
    Case and Operating Structure......................81

    4.2.2   Define Shared Goals and Key
    Success Factors...81

    4.2.3   Define Operating Rules and
    Responsibilities..82

    4.2.4   Blueprinting the Memorandum of
    Understanding (MOU) 83

4.3   Consortium Formation – Key Steps 84

4.4   Checklist – Common Concerns
During Pre-consortium Agreement 88

Chapter 5.0   Consortium Governance...91

5.1   Overview 91

    5.1.1   Rethinking Traditional
    Governance Model 92

5.2   What is Blockchain Consortium Governance?........93

5.3   Why is Good Governance Necessary for a
Blockchain Consortium? 93

5.4   Components of a Blockchain
Consortium Governance 95

5.5 Scaling Up the Blockchain Consortiums
Through Robust Governance 98
5.6 Blockchain Consortium Governance Models..........99
5.7 Facets of Blockchain Consortium Governance......103
5.8 Blockchain Consortiums Risk Factors 110
5.9 Blockchain Consortium's Challenges...................114
5.10 Blockchain Consortiums Collaborative
Governance Model – Suggestive Framework.........119
5.11 Rapid Checklist for Effective
Consortium Governance Establishment 121

Chapter 6.0 Making Business Sense of Blockchain Consortium ... 125

6.1 Overview – Business Model for Consortiums.......125
6.2 Consortium Opportunity Analysis –
Business Model Canvas 126
6.3 Consortium Business Model Canvas 131

**Chapter 7.0 Blockchain Consortium – Readiness
Assessment Tool.. 133**

**Chapter 8.0 Conclusion – Prepare Now, Beware of
Promises and Look at the Facts 141**

8.1 Factors Desirable in a Blockchain Consortium 142
8.1.1 Digitized Documents..............................143
8.1.2 Workflow Automation 143
8.1.3 Application Programming Interface (API)....144
8.1.4 Web User Interface (UI) 144
8.1.5 Standards...145
8.1.6 Interoperability.......................................145
8.1.7 Convergence of Blockchain, Internet of
Things (IoT) and Artificial
Intelligence (AI)......................................151
8.2 Key Learnings for Future
Consortium Participants..153

Annexure – (A)   ***Top Blockchain Consortiums –***
         Detailed Overview **157**

   1. *Tradelens*...*157*
   2. *MOBI (Mobility Open Blockchain Initiative)*..........*158*
   3. *Energy Web Foundation (EWF)*..............................*159*
   4. *FoodTrust*..*161*
   5. *We. Trade*..*162*
   6. *Oil and Gas Consortium (OOC)*..........................*163*
   7. *B3I – Blockchain Insurance Industry Initiative*........*164*
   8. *Risk Block* *165*
   9. *Global Shipping Business Network (GSBN)* *166*
  10. *Marco Polo*..*168*
  11. *Synaptic Health Alliance* *169*
  12. *Contour* *170*
  13. *Komgo* *171*
  14. *eTradeConnect*...*172*
  15. *MineHub*...*173*
  16. *Financial Blockchain Shenzhen Consortium*.............*174*
  17. *India Trade Connect* *175*
  18. *PharmaLedger*..*176*

Annexure – (B)   ***List of other Consortiums*** **179**

   1. *GLBC Global Legal Blockchain Consortium*
     https://legalconsortium.org/ *179*
   2. *CULegder: https://www.culedger.com/* *180*
   3. *Decentralized Identity Foundation (DIF) –*
     https://identity.foundation/ *180*
   4. *Integrated Engineering Blockchain*
     Consortium (IEBC) – https://iebc.co/ *181*
   5. *Retail Blockchain Consortium (RBC) –*
     https://www.retailBlockchainconsortium.org/ *182*
   6. *Tracr – https://www.tracr.com/*...........................*183*
   7. *Clipeum* *183*

8. *BankChain – https://www.bankchaintech.com/* *184*

9. *Bay Area Trade Finance Blockchain Platform (BATFB)* *184*

10. *Global Trade Connectivity Network – www.mas.gov.sg/development/fintech/ trade-finance* *185*

11. *Fnality – https://www.fnality.org/* *185*

12. *DELIVER* *186*

13. *Blockchain Interoperability Alliance (BIA)* *186*

14. *The Coupon Bureau (https://www.thecouponbureau.org/)* *187*

15. *Trusted IoT Alliance (https://www.iiconsortium.org/)* *188*

Annexure – (C)   **Project Ubin Sets the Bar for Central Banks Looking to Adopt Blockchain**............................ *189*

Annexure – (D)   **Interoperability Examples** *195*

References... *199*

Glossary of Important Questions *205*

Preface

More than a decade has passed since the world has known the revolutionary Blockchain technology. During that time, the promise of what Blockchain can offer businesses has evolved from a cryptocurrency payment gateway platform to something that's bigger and truly a game changer. Because Blockchain has the potential to drive a distributed and decentralized way of re-imagining processes and business models, it can be a transformative technology for many businesses. However, many business and technology leaders may overlook its potential usage and value for their business and industry, or primarily associate it with Bitcoin and cryptocurrency applications.

Although the initial hype is being replaced with growing scepticism and caution, it is still common for business leaders, especially CIOs, to be under pressure from their executive leadership to address Blockchain. Unreasonable, hype-fuelled expectations should be addressed through awareness and education. However, joining a consortium is a way forward for most senior leadership teams to demonstrate that they are proactively addressing Blockchain. This also helps shift risk to the broader consortium so that it does not rest solely with the CIOs.

While Blockchain Consortiums have enjoyed growth in absolute member numbers, Gartner estimates that fewer than 2% of enterprises worldwide are participating in Blockchain Consortiums at any level. In 2020, the C-Suite is looking forward to invest more money and resources behind Blockchain as a strategic solution in more meaningful and tangible ways. Today's

Blockchain Consortiums are established in an emerging, technologically changing market. We are in the "big bang" of the Blockchain universe, a complex and sometimes chaotic world. In this uncertain environment the consortiums' needs lean heavily towards organization, community building and education. Consortiums will continue to grow as the technology becomes more established and mature. They will focus more on ecosystems, platforms, and products and we are already seeing this type of movement and growth.

Consortiums are also attempting to address, on a war footing, interoperability between different Blockchain types, as this aspect will be critical for mainstream adoption of Blockchain. Along with that, consortiums are also focusing parallelly on other aspects such as user experience, integration with legacy systems, and ecosystem development.

Today, business leaders need to ask themselves whether they are ready to accept and adopt the changes that joining a Blockchain Consortium will require of their organizations. And also, are these changes worth the returns? While searching for accurate, ground-level, unbiased, and business-oriented information to answer the above questions, we realized that there is no single repository or a detailed guide that gives complete information or best practices about Blockchain Consortiums. It was this obvious lack of information that inspired us to put together this handbook for Blockchain practitioners and business leaders, to guide them and help plan their participation in a holistic way by avoiding the hype and focusing on the core Value Propositions that Blockchain Consortiums may unlock for their organizations.

Acknowledgements

It was an inspiring effort to compile in one book, all the information regarding Blockchain Consortiums – and a very challenging task as well. We had to identify the right sources and exact details (scattered across multiple sources), then bring them all together in one place from a truly pragmatic and business value perspective. It took the collective wisdom and the more than three decades of technology and business leadership experience, years of Blockchain technology expertise, and the experience of hundreds of customer interactions, that we three authors have. It was an expedition that was absolutely rewarding.

We would like to thank all industry leading platforms, technology companies, consultancies and thought leaders, for working on building and supporting the ecosystem and for making efforts to educate and guide us.

They have inspired us to put together a comprehensive guide by leveraging all of our experiences and backgrounds in IT and Business Management.

About the Authors

Varun V Singhi

(https://www.linkedin.com/in/singhi)

Blockchain Business Strategy Enthusiast

Asia School of Business & MIT Sloan Alumni

An alumnus from MIT Sloan's partnership program Asia School of Business, Varun Singhi is an experienced Database Strategy and Business Transformation Professional with 11+ years of expertise across US and APAC regions in strategizing, leading and implementing technology solutions for businesses to move forward and bringing a unique perspective, execution and operational capabilities for digital business transformation initiatives. He has done various strategy consulting projects for clients in South East Asian countries. He is deeply interested in the cutting-edge research of disruptive technologies and a passionate Blockchain explorer. He is a certified Blockchain expert and fond of training and talent development activities. He has conducted many seminars for Universities, Government, and the private sector on Blockchain and its use cases. He is adept in Digital Strategy and Transformation, Stakeholder and Vendor Management, Business development and data driven analysis. His global work experience and acquired business acumen knowledge enables him to bring customer-centric mindfulness to the firm by creating tangible value.

Varun also serves as a mentor for a few startups in education and non-profit sectors in India.

Prior to his MBA, he worked as a technology professional, primarily implementing Oracle's suite of products mainly ERP software and Relational database technologies. He has worked with system integrators like Wipro, Cognizant, DXC for global clients such as Cisco, Pearson Education and State Street, in United States.

Murthy Chitlur

(https://www.linkedin.com/in/murthychitlur)

Chief Executive Officer, Tangensys Technologies Pvt. Ltd.

B.E. (SIT Tumkur 1991-95)

Murthy Chitlur is a Senior Management professional with extensive leadership experience currently spearheading the operations of Tangensys Technologies as the CEO. He is also an advisory member for Ether Daylight Systems Pvt Ltd, Arohaka Technologies Pvt Ltd and Snipe Tech Pvt Ltd for emerging technologies. Before taking up entrepreneurship, he has worked for 20+ years in India and the USA in with expertise in Service Delivery, Product Development, Capability Development, Continuous Improvement, Pre-sales, Consulting, Client Management, Organization Change Management and Leadership Development. He has also worked in the Centre of Excellence ('CoE') leadership with 12 years' overseas experience in various client engagement roles in the USA.

Murthy is an expert in improving team performance while securing customer loyalty and forging valuable relationships with internal and external partners. He has worked with big firms such as Intel, AOL, and has also consulted for global clients such as WellPoint (Anthem), HSBC, Caremark, Mattel, ABB, Blue Cross Blue Shield, SAAB and FAB on domains like healthcare, insurance, energy, mortgages, e-commerce, online games, internet service and media, CRM, banking and manufacturing.

Murthy specializes in Blockchain Consulting and Product (PoC and Concept) Development, and one of his core strength is ability to set up and lead global teams.

Srinivas Mahankali

(https://www.linkedin.com/in/srini-nisg)

Principal Consultant (Blockchain)

National Institute for Smart Government

B.Tech. (IIT Chennai 1984-88), MBA (IIM Bangalore 1988-90)

An alumnus of IIT Madras and IIM Bangalore, Srinivas Mahankali is presently a Principal Consultant at NISG's Blockchain Centre of Excellence in a Government and NASSCOM owned organization, NISG (National Institute for Smart Government), where he plays a key role in the promotion and implementation of Blockchain projects across the Public Sector and Government. He is certified in Lean Six Sigma, NCFM Level 2, Capital Markets and R3 Corda.

Prior to this, he was leading the Blockchain Centre of Excellence at ULTS (ULCCS Group, Calicut, Kerala), leading a pool of Blockchain experts in executing solutions for Enterprise and Educational applications.

He also led Strategy and IT for three years at Apollo LogiSolutions (ALS), India's leading integrated logistics services company. Here, he formulated and implemented the ABEX (Apollo Business Excellence) program, and executed a comprehensive overhaul of IT hardware, networking and ERP management at ALS. During his tenure as CIO, ALS won the awards, 'The Best Integrated Logistics Services Company' and 'Best Logistics CEO in India' in 2017. He has authored and co-authored two prominent books 'Blockchain – The Untold Story' and 'AI & ML Powered Agents of Automation and Successful Organizations in Action', respectively. His book 'Blockchain – The Untold Story' is the first ever book to be translated from English into Chinese by Artificial Engineering Bots.

His latest books are 'Blockchain for Non-IT Professionals' and 'Corona Wars'.

Blockchain – The World of Decentralization

1.1 Introduction

> Blockchain is as significant now as the internet was 25 years ago.
>
> Blythe Masters, Former CEO of the Digital Holdings

The last three years has seen a rapid change in the world's understanding of and approach towards Blockchain, the new technological paradigm that has hit the world. It is now clear to almost anyone that Blockchain not only offers solutions for the many risks being faced by an increasingly centralized and digital world but is also catalyzing a refreshing change in the way we work and respond to events. A democratic, decentralized, distributed and tamper-proof, immutable ledger can help startups with innumerable compliance tracking issues and empower them to collaborate for collective success. Efforts to achieve the United Nations' Sustainable Development Goals can also get a big boost with the help of Blockchain.

By acting as a Trusted Third Party in a programmatic manner, Blockchain is bringing in unforeseen trusted interactions, elimination of non-value adding middlemen. This is leading to increased efficiencies, affordability, lower costs and a vastly improved environment that offers, pure and authentic interactions, products, services and information for customer delight. Blockchain offers these possibilities by abstracting a number of technology paradigms that are simple in nature and combining them beautifully.

Blockchain is a technology that is poised to usher in a new way of conducting business that will change everyday life for the better. Blockchain empowers groups of organizations to produce better outcomes by creating new growth opportunities that together are greater than the feats that any single member can achieve alone. Businesses and many governments across the world are finding new use cases of Blockchain every day and it is only a matter of a few more years for us to be totally used to patronizing any service or product that is able to demonstrate its authenticity and purity, an essential feature of a Blockchain solution.

1.2 Origin and Definition of Blockchain

How it all started — The origin of Blockchain technology sounds just like the plot of an incredible epic thriller. It all started with a nine-page whitepaper publication introducing a decentralized peer-to-peer electronic cash system called "Bitcoin" under the onscreen fictitious name of Satoshi Nakamoto by an anonymous scientist in 2008. Satoshi 's work outlines in detail how to create a whole new cryptocurrency based on a sophisticated mathematical formula and a resilient distributed architecture.

Most people who have heard of Blockchain associate it with the Bitcoin cryptocurrency. Though the two are related, they are not the same. The Bitcoin protocol that was launched on January 3, 2009, was the first known application of Blockchain technology and it provided a reliable solution for achieving a consensus in distributed systems that create and transact value over the internet without fear of "double-spending".

This problem was formulated into a story called the 'Byzantine General's Problem' where a group of nine generals decided to attack a fort they were surrounding, subject to the majority's decision, despite being handicapped by improper communication facilities. 25-years after the problem's formulation, Bitcoin successfully demonstrated a solution for computer systems to achieve Byzantine tolerance even in the face of a sizeable number of adversaries and adverse conditions.

Bitcoin Blockchain is a living example to show that although this this technology is often questioned and misunderstood, it is a new paradigm that has come to stay with us in the long term. Bitcoin, the first successful implementation of Blockchain technology consists of six primary elements:

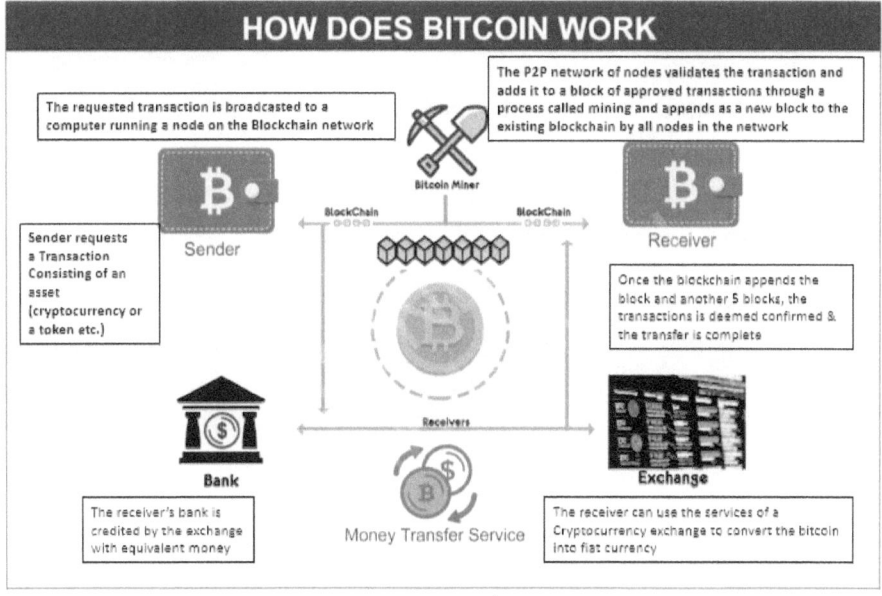

Fig 1.1 – How Does Bitcoin Work?

a. An updated distributed ledger replicated across all the peers undertaking transactions through the platform, consisting of the updated status of Unspent Outputs (UTXO) in chronological order.

b. A network of nodes undertaking to verify and propagate the transactions generated by the participants.

c. A group of miners dispersed across the world to mine the transactions to ensure the authenticity of the same, maintaining the integrity of the Blockchain for all times to come, using an automated execution of the protocol defined by the consensus algorithm called 'Proof-of-Work.' 'Proof-of-Work' represents the amount of work that the miners undertake by utilizing their computing power and electricity spent, to be eligible for block rewards in the form of newly mined coins as per a predefined formula.

d. Blockchain wallets used by the participants to initiate transactions and store the value in the form of UTXOs or unspent transaction outputs measured in the number of Bitcoins.

e. The value that is exchanged across the platform, namely the 'Bitcoin' or its fraction, is treated as a cryptocurrency with all the properties that we associate with the fiat currency in the real world, except for the unitized physical representation and regulatory approvals.

f. Exchanges that facilitate the buying and selling of cryptocurrencies and derived products known as tokens among themselves using wallets, and the conversion of the same into fiat currencies in a dynamic manner.

Bitcoin has proved that billions of dollars' worth of value can be exchanged across the world from one person to another unknown person, without the need of a trusted central party – a bank or government in this case. As of July 2020, over 18.4 million Bitcoins with an approximate total value of over 171 billion US Dollar at a unit price of over 9,200 US Dollars are in circulation. The success of Bitcoin led to the launch of several variations of alternate Blockchains for a variety of purposes. The majority of them are cryptocurrencies with different properties in terms of privacy, speed of execution, consensus mechanism for transaction validation – the most prominent variation was proposed in the form of the Ethereum Blockchain platform by Vitalik Buterin and his team at Ethereum foundation. Ethereum allowed businesses to create decentralized versions of real-life applications that we see in the day-to-day world through the implementation of 'Smart Contracts' which are programs created to replicate the business agreements into applications that can be run on Blockchain databases.

Over the years, the cost of infrastructure in the form of storage space and processing power required for IT applications has come down substantially. The availability of high-quality Cloud service providers has reduced the need for investments in high cost, on-premises infrastructure. Approaches like 'Open source technologies', decentralized methodologies and 'Pay-as-you-go services' are clubbed together to facilitate the deployment of cutting-edge technology and powered infrastructure to find new solutions to our problems, rather cheaply. Messaging Protocols, Event-driven communication and record updation, API (Application Programming Interfaces) are facilitating collaboration between applications across multiple on-Premise and Cloud-based applications seamlessly. IBM, Microsoft, Oracle, Amazon and many leading organizations are offering high-end secure IT applications, including Blockchain, as a service that can facilitate the large-scale implementation of automation enabling technologies in a convenient and cost-effective manner.

1.2.1 Resilient Data Structures of Blockchain

We have seen that in the traditional approach, the participants in a typical business scenario pretty much operate in silos and all the parties are connected to the centralized big market place or to the dominant player who connects the buyers and sellers or provides services to the clients globally.

In contrast to this, Blockchain presents an inter-enterprise scenario that offers a 'Single Source of Truth' where all the peers are connected to each other with a possibility to conduct peer-to-peer transactions as per business logic codified in the form of Smart Contracts. The dominant player, while being the facilitator, could still be a player whose returns depend on the quantity and quality of the business happening on the network.

The Single Point of Failure (SPOF) has always been the bane of most centralized organizations which maintain their databases under a single command, control and administration. This is the weakness that is most often exploited by the ransomware virus creators who were behind some of the most lethal attacks on global organizations by unleashing the WannaCry virus.

While distributed and shared databases also help in non-repudiation by the parties undertaking transactions, the ability to reconstruct the database from other members of the network eliminates the risk of the SPOF from the very route, thus blunting the weapons of the cybercriminals. This minimizes the risk by tilting the RRR (Risk-Reward-Ratio) away from the investors in these crooked instruments.

Thus, Blockchain is seen as the vehicle for safe and secure automation at scale.

Enterprise Blockchain platforms like Hyperledger Fabric, Quorum, etc. were developed as variations of the Ethereum platform while enterprise applications such as Multichain and R3 Corda took inspiration from the architecture and other elements of Bitcoin Blockchain. Blockchain converts the traditional internet infrastructure as we know through its TCP/IP protocol from the Internet of Information to the Internet of Value, by acting as a Trusted Third Party to any peer-to-peer interactions. The features of Blockchain that facilitate this are shown in the following figure. Blockchain Combines Encryption, Encoding, Hashing, Public Key Infrastructure (PKI), Timestamps, DSA and Broadcast for the Internet of Value by bringing Privacy, Permission, Password Management within the reach of an individual peer and frees him/her from dependence on the

Trust Anchors who have now grown unduly large, leading to a centralized internet.

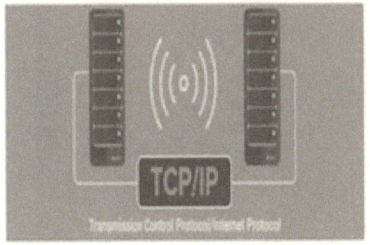

How Blockchain changes the game for the Digital era participants

Problems:
- Open communication
- Meant for only information exchange
- No encryption
- Prone to Data breach
- Low trust protocol

Blockchain offers : Encryption, Permission & Access rights, Smart contract capability, Privacy using ZK SNARK, Homomorphic encryptions.

Leads to secure conditional trading of data and value at scale & Trust between unknown entities

- Resulting in **Internet of Value** Versus **Internet of Information**
- Blockchain makes IoT devices Safe and Secure to operate
- Blockchain offers high quality data for AI/ML applications & increase ROI on Analytics investments

DISINTERMEDIATING TRUST – EMPOWERING INDIVIDUAL USERS – FACILITATING P2P TRANSACTIONS

Fig 1.2 – How Blockchain changes the game for digital era participants

Blockchain combines existing technologies – cryptography and programmatic concepts like encryption, encoding and hashing in a unique manner to achieve amazing benefits offering a new paradigm of trusted disintermediated transactions. Next, we are going to describe in detail, some of the technical components involved in Blockchain technology. So, for those who are from a non-technical background and are reading this, it might sound a bit daunting but it is okay to not understand this in detail. Just knowing the terminology is good, but if you are feeling adventurous, then we definitely recommend that you understand every component in detail to get more comfortable with Blockchain technology.

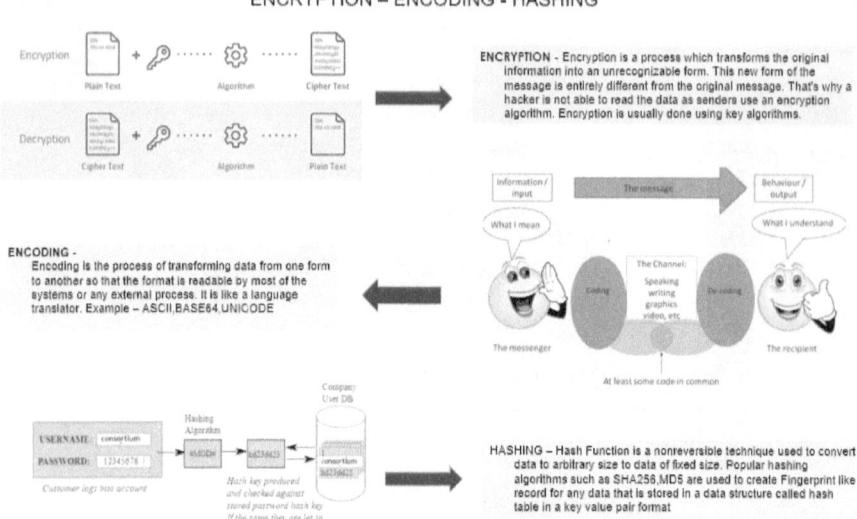

Fig 1.3 – Encryption – Encoding – Hashing

I. **Hash function**: A hash function produces a unique output for a given input, which cannot be replicated. Hash of any information is treated as the unique and indisputable representation of the information. Hashes form the heart of Blockchain as the blocks are represented by the hash of the information and are chained together as a linked list of chronologically mined and validated blocks.

II. **Merkle root (Root of roots)**: While a hash is a unique number derived out of the base number, the Merkle root is derived from hashing pairs of transactions together until only one element is left. Since the hash was unique, a change in any transaction will result in a change in the Merkle root, which can be easily caught.

III. **Public Key Infrastructure (PKI):** To facilitate secure electronic transmission of information and undertake ultra-safe transactions, Blockchain employs several cryptographic applications. PKI is a set of technological procedures used to create, manage, distribute, use, store, and revoke digital certificates. PKI is used to authenticate participating parties using public keys and corresponding private keys connected to each other through complex algorithmic relations, requiring rigorous proofs to confirm identities for facilitating information exchange. PKI uses X.509 certificates to identify the owners of public keys.

    a. **Private Key and Public Key**: The Private Key and Public Key are used to encrypt information using mathematical algorithms, rendering decryption virtually impossible without these keys. Computationally, it is similar to the factoring of prime numbers, which is a simple, mathematical procedure. However, decomposing the result is difficult without prior knowledge of its factors.

    b. **RSA Algorithm:** PKI systems normally use RSA algorithms for linking Public Keys and Private Keys. RSA (Revest–Shamir–Adleman) is one of the first Public Key cryptosystems and is widely used for secure data transmission. In such a cryptosystem, the encryption key is public and it is different from the decryption key which is kept secret (private).

    c. **Elliptic Curve Digital Signature (ECDSA) Algorithm:** Blockchain systems use Elliptical curve cryptography to issue secure Public Key Private Key pairs. The messages are encrypted by a digital signature algorithm namely, ECDSA that ensures that only authorized owners of targeted messages can securely decrypt the messages.

IV. **Digital Signatures:** Digital signatures are a unique aspect of Blockchain transactions and provide a layer of security to carry out and validate genuine transactions. A digital signature is a mathematical scheme to present the authenticity of digital messages or documents. A valid digital signature gives the recipient reason to believe that the message was created by a known sender (authentication), and that the sender cannot deny having sent the message (non-repudiation), or that the message was not altered in transit.

V. **Consensus Mechanisms:** The mechanism by which members come to an agreement about the authenticity of a transaction is referred to as the 'Consensus Mechanism.' Consensus formation ensures the involvement of multiple validators in a systematic and predetermined manner, ensuring decentralization and objectivity of decision making. It ensures implementation of the key features of the Blockchain platform like increased trust, immutability of the transactions, and maintenance of the integrity of the platform. The consensus mechanism is the soul of the Blockchain platform and has to help members in reaching the right decision all the time. The sanctity of the Blockchain application depends on the strength and reliability of the consensus mechanism. The consensus mechanism followed by Bitcoin and the earlier version of the public Ethereum client is known as 'Proof-of-Work (POW)' where miners or validators compete with each other and burn valuable resources like computing power and enormous amounts of electricity to guess the right Nonce (number used only once) and create a targeted hash to win the race to create a block. POW – followed by Bitcoin Blockchain and some versions of Ethereum Blockchain – consumes a huge amount of resources to arrive at a deterministic consensus. The Ethereum platform will soon shift to a 'Proof of Stake (PoS)'- based consensus, which involves negligible energy consumption.

Some new-generation public platforms use variations of 'POW' – and 'POS'- based consensus algorithms like Proof of Elapsed Time (PoET) and Delegated Proof of Stake (DPOS) to minimize resource utilization and wastage. Enterprise Blockchains use energy-efficient algorithms like 'Proof of Authority' (POA), Practical Byzantine Fault-Tolerant' (PBFT), 'Node to Node' (N2N) and their variations to arrive at a deterministic consensus.

The figure below describes Blockchain's Magical Components:

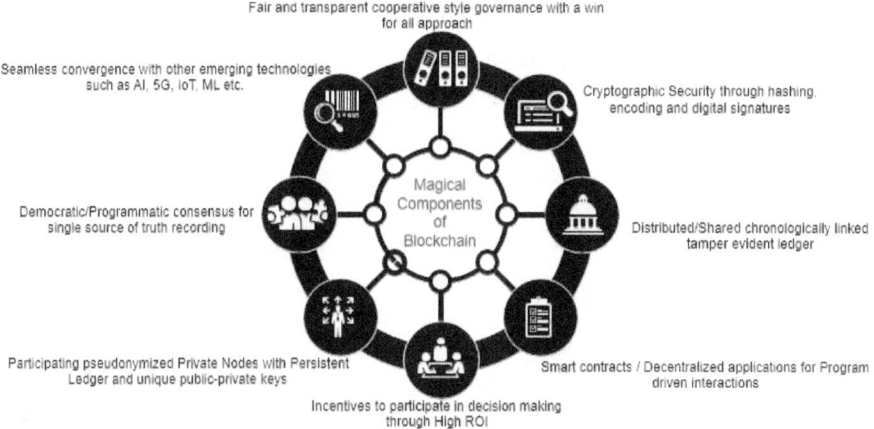

Fig 1.4 – Magical Components of Blockchain

As seen in the above section, the discovery of the Blockchain paradigm has been achieved by an ingenious combination of the various simple tools and techniques that have been in vogue for decades. Let us now define Blockchain with our understanding of the various components, features and benefits offered by this unique technology.

What is Blockchain? Formally, Blockchain is a digital mechanism to create a distributed digital ledger on which two or more participants in a peer-to-peer network can exchange information and assets directly without the need for a trusted intermediary. This facilitation of trustless transactions is achieved by using advanced cryptography to secure the identities of participants in the network, undertaking time-stamped, immutable transactions with decentralized processing to exchange data and change ownership of assets using Smart Contracts which further provides transparency, tamper resistance, auditability and enhanced trust through the system acting as a Trusted Third Party in Triple entry-accounting.

What are Smart Contracts? Contracts that specify the terms and conditions of doing business. In Blockchain, those terms are captured in the technology of the Blockchain itself as a Smart Contract – lines of code that capture and execute the business rules and agreements of a Blockchain. The rules allow the Blockchain to execute transactions without human intervention. Smart Contracts abstract real-life business agreements into applications on a decentralized network of computers running on Ethereum.

Traditionally, enterprises are used to centralized databases such as Oracle, Microsoft SQL Server for storing data which utilizes CRUD (Create, Read, Update and Delete) principle for manipulating data. In general, Blockchain databases can be considered SALT databases as per the context. In the context of Permissioned Blockchain systems, SALT may be described as:

- **Sequenced** (time-stamped),

- **Agreed** (decided in a manner agreeable to the participants as per an approved program)

- **Ledgered** (maintained in a database of key-value pairs reflecting the state of ownership of assets)

- **Tamper resistant** (almost impossible to change the order of the records committed).

The important feature of this Blockchain approach is the 'decentralized' approach where the decision regarding the correctness of the transactions is taken without recourse to an individual entity's authority and muscle power. The transactions with due approvals and authorizations representing the real-life scenario are sent to a pool of network managers, who can then collectively follow a designated approach and vote on the transactions to be included in the approved chain of events that influence the records and ledgers permanently.

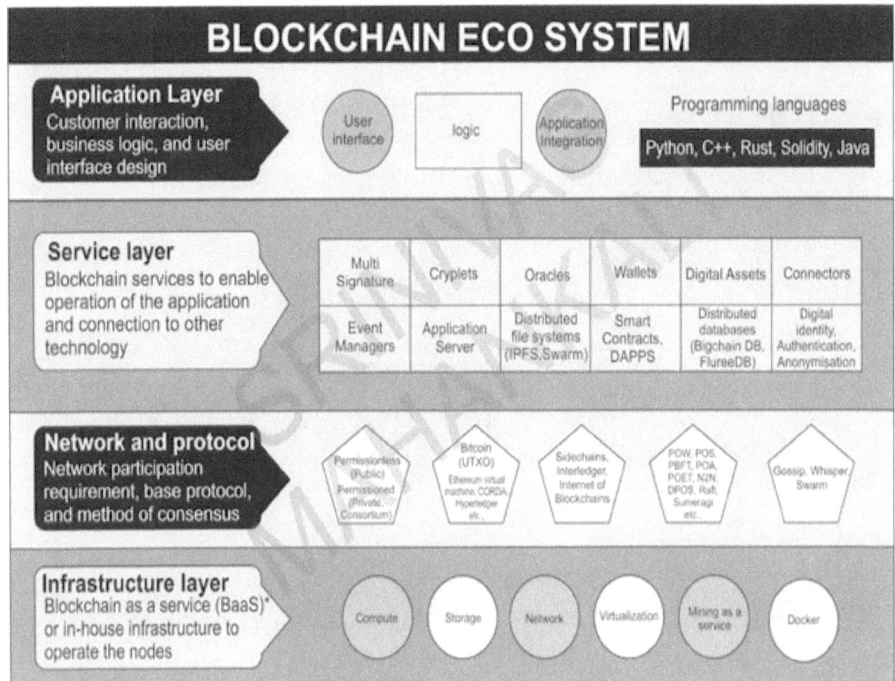

Fig 1.5 – An integrated representation of different components of Blockchain ecosystem

While the existing incumbents involved in running businesses across governments are comfortable with centralized approaches, the choice of a decentralized approach and Distributed Ledger Technology for the future is seen as a decision that may yield substantial returns, but is fraught with unforeseen risks. As the technology is still in an early stage of adoption, several factors need to be considered by the decision makers before they undertake to migrate to the new paradigm. The following table gives a bird's eye view of the aspects to be considered for evaluating the suitability of a Distributed Ledger Technology-based solution:

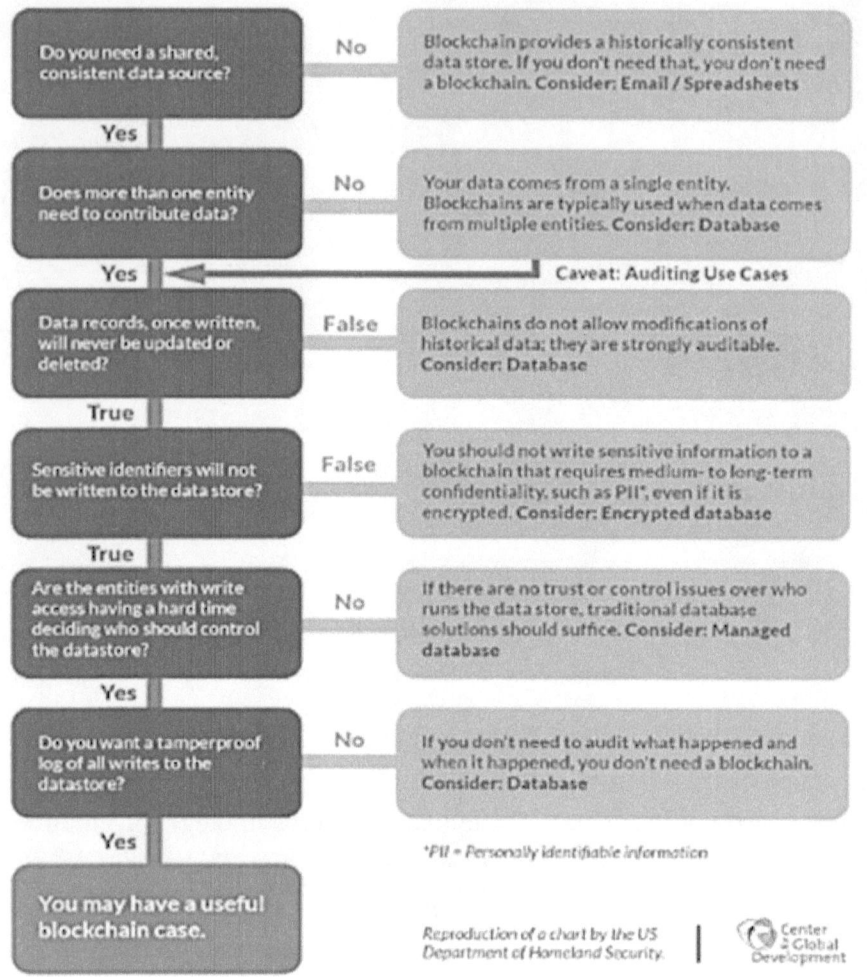

Fig 1.6 – Do you need a Blockchain? Decision flow chart
Source: Centre for Global Development

A high-powered committee with the involvement of the top management professionals should consider and analyze the various aspects of the problems to be tacked and evaluate potential solutions.

1.3 Applications of Blockchain Technology

Blockchain's key applications can well be summarized in the following figure:

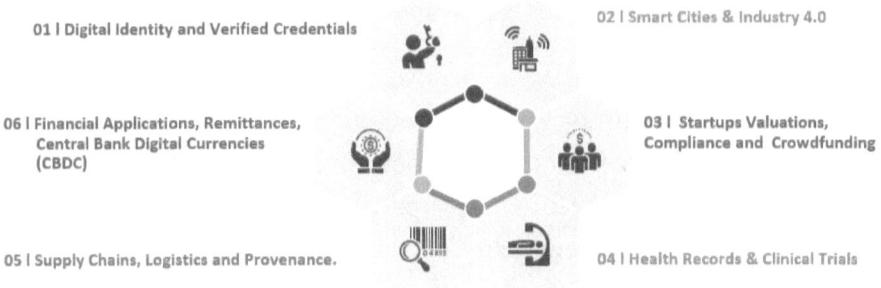

Multi Dimensions of Blockchain Applications

01 I Digital Identity and Verified Credentials

02 I Smart Cities & Industry 4.0

06 I Financial Applications, Remittances, Central Bank Digital Currencies (CBDC)

03 I Startups Valuations, Compliance and Crowdfunding

05 I Supply Chains, Logistics and Provenance.

04 I Health Records & Clinical Trials

Fig 1.7 – Multiple Dimensions of Blockchain Applications

1.4 Blockchain's Value Proposition Across Industries and Use Cases

a) **Government and Public Sector**

Problem: Governments offer numerous certificates of identification and authenticity to their citizens. They are the biggest spenders of public money, collectors of taxes and distributors of subsidies. Governments also undertake large projects on an ongoing basis inside the country and outside the country through the External Affairs Ministry. Governments must implement Smart City projects and provide cybersecurity to critical installations. All these areas are fraught with complexity and potential fraud, leading to a lot of data leakage and loss of money on a huge scale.

Solution offered by Blockchain: By offering foolproof methods for issuing unique digital identities, ensuring the provenance of goods and supplies, providing certificates registered on a Blockchain and ensuring accountability and transparency in project management, procurement, vendor management and supply chains through non-refutable digital signatures and immutably stored data that cannot be manipulated and modified, governments stand to save a huge portion of their expenses while delighting citizens. After all, citizens demand transparency, efficiency, ease of interaction and lower costs that Blockchain's dis-intermediated trust can offer as a de facto outcome.

b) Project Management

Problems: Project management involves the delivery of expected and planned outcomes through the utilization of defined and budgeted resources consisting of money, manpower, materials and time. This involves interaction between multiple parties both inside and extraneous to organizations, and the results are dependent on multiple parties working strictly in consonance with their contracts regarding implementation. Most often, the lack of synchronization between the parties concerned, and participants falling short of their deliverables leads to cost and time overruns and humongous losses, throwing all plans awry.

Solution offered by Blockchain: Recording the contracts, monitoring the project status and adherence to deliverables in the same manner by all the parties concerned, as per the milestones, is best done over a Blockchain platform to ensure compliance. Cryptographic references to project status are stored in the Blockchain and the status report with respect to the deliverables is shared periodically – and, on critical matters, is shared over the Distributed Ledgers in real-time. The 'tamper-evident' nature of the records and the 'Triple entry-accounting' feature of the Blockchain acting as a Trusted Third Party, ensures that the accountability of all concerned parties is monitored in a foolproof manner for timely action, and also, to dispense rewards/penalties required to put the projections execution ahead of schedule on all dimensions. Transparent procurement, process-automated bid management with details of successful vendors is recorded on a Blockchain, and monitoring the progress of their deliveries can also trigger delivery versus payments in a trusted manner, with the highest accountability of the involved officials, thus eliminating chances for errors and misappropriation.

c) Digital Identity

Problems: Multiple records, Duplication of efforts and processes, Siloed systems and potential for identity fraud and stolen credential copies.

Solution offered by Blockchain: Issue and verify once on Blockchain, link multiple identities to a unique Blockchain identity – operated through a single user interface or a digital wallet. This eliminates the need for multiple verifications across establishments thus saving a lot of time, effort and documentation which maximizes the trustworthiness of the identity information.

d) Voting

Problem: Tedious manual paper and print-intensive processes requiring humongous funds and fake/unaccounted identities, pose enormous challenges for countries and enterprises undertaking elections for governing bodies and on-board resolutions.

Solution offered by Blockchain: By uniquely identifying voters in a foolproof manner and recording their votes through their digital signatures through a verifiable and non-refutable system, Blockchain eliminates fake votes, wrong votes and extensive paperwork, eliminating wasteful processes to reduce costs enormously.

e) Registries and Certificates

Problem: Fake certificates and the high cost and time required for their verification, plague the documentation of events from birth to will execution for asset acquisition and credential accumulation.

Solution offered by Blockchain: Educational, Municipal, Police and other credential certificates can be issued and shared securely eliminating fakes and offering benefits for instant audit and reconciliation while establishing clear title.

f) Benefits and Subsidy Distribution

Problem: Fake claims, excessive middle layers leading to leakages and adding non-value costs drain valuable resources of governments and trusts.

Solution offered by Blockchain: Clear identification of beneficiaries, allotment and monitoring of benefit utilization for every unit issued with minimal intermediary intervention in near real-time allows for high productivity of welfare spends.

g) Supply Chain

Problem: Procurement: Subjectivity and opaque procurement processes create leakages and mistrust. Financial Documentation: Letter of Credit, Suppliers credit and other financial transactions offer a lot of scope for manipulation and mistrust. Provenance: Fake goods and false claims of being premium, hamper a variety of products including pharmaceuticals, food, imported, exported and specialized products. Retail: Warranty claims and Loyalty rewards cross multiple vendors are difficult to track and often lead to disputes. Transport conditions: Un-monitored cold-storage transported goods like pharmaceuticals, food, milk and dairy products lead to the consumption of spurious/expired products.

Solution offered by Blockchain: Transparent and trusted processes offered by an immutable, shared ledger of records between verified identities. Digital signatures for non-repudiation and a shared ledger for near-real-time communication drastically reduce costs and the scope for fraud. Smart Contracts triggered to capture events like a change of ownership and transfer of assets immutably on a shared ledger, help identify the origin of the products along with certifications of originality of standard adherence, especially valuable in automotive spares. Blockchain facilitates the seamless tracking of warranty claims and allotted rewards until redemption, for increased effectiveness and for the benefit of consumers. By recording the temperature of cold-storage items across the supply chain and tracking them on a Blockchain ledger, the consignment details of spoiled items can be quickly traced. This minimizes the opportunities for wilful manipulation.

h) Healthcare

Problem: Fake drugs, compliances in clinical record management, health record tracking and the settlement of insurance claims often trigger fraud and manipulation.

Solution offered by Blockchain: Blockchain can offer multiple benefits for solving the various challenges of healthcare domains like the seamless management of EHRs with utmost privacy and security features, transparent compliance tracking in case of clinical records, and insurance settlement and origin-to-chemist tracking of pharmaceutical goods, etc.

i) Smart City

Problem: Unauthorized access by cybercriminals to leverage net connectivity of the Internet of Things (IoT) devices for DDOS attacks and illegal actions like crypto-jacking, data leaks, etc. The command and control of autonomous vehicles and drones need to be secured against cybercriminals.

Solution offered by Blockchain: Blockchain offers a protective shield for IoT Gateways, autonomous vehicles, drones, and robots and prevents unauthorized access by criminals and manipulators. This enables secured automation. Blockchain facilitates accurate assessment of renewable energy claims and peer-to-peer energy trading among prosumers.

Further, Blockchain has extensive uses in a Smart City scenario in securing:

- Smart healthcare
- Smart transportation
- Smart energy
- Smart government
- Smart tourism
- Smart education
- Smart environmental protection

j) Cybersecurity

Problems: Single points of failure of centralized management offer valuable targets for cybercriminals. Increasing digitization and billions of internet connections managed by centralized systems run the risk of derailment and ransom attacks. WannaCry, one such virus that infected 230,000 computers in over 150 countries, using 20 different languages cost US $300 per computer, to decrypt and release the data.

Solution offered by Blockchain: By distributing data across multiple ledgers, authenticating identities and encrypting transaction information, Blockchain offers a de-risking mechanism for data-intensive applications and blunts the designs of Ransomware criminals who fraudulently sneak into corporate systems, encrypt the data and demand a ransom to decrypt the same.

k) Eliminating Fake Certificates and Identities

The utility of Blockchain in eliminating fakes through a trusted document management and verification source to destination ownership tracking can be succinctly summarized in the following lifecycle activities that can be authentically stored on a Blockchain:

- Cradle to Grave/Womb to Tomb – All certificates in one's life from birth certificates, vaccination records, health/property and academic, non-academic and identity records, legal will recording and execution, etc., need impeccable tracking that Blockchain provides.

- From Dispute to Trust – Any agreements and compliance issues can be easily reconciled.

- Farm to Fork/Catch to Consumption – Safe and compassionate handling of animals and amphibians meant for consumption can be tracked through the supply chain.

- Procure to Pay – Complete transparency in the procurement process by recording activities at every stage. Procurement is the biggest source of subjective behaviour that can be made transparent.

- Pay to Cash – Manpower and work-outsourcing organizations can minimize Pay-Bill cycle leakages through instant settlements and eliminating the need for reconciliation.

- Admission to Retirement – Academic and non-academic certificates and transcripts can be stored and shared privately without any fear of fake certificates and time loss.

- Segregation of Duties: In issues of project management or execution of shared responsibilities in organizations, IT projects and new product development, there is a need for responsible and automated tracking of the discharge of one's duties. Digital signatures and non-repudiation help in achieving instant confirmations and recognition of good and productive behaviour.

- Start-up valuation and compliance tracking: Most small companies suffer from the inability to capture valuable contributions and tracking from the promoters and investors. Blockchain enables perfect, real-time valuation, promoter shares' tracking and support in compliance management for the start-up founders, from the idea stage itself.

- Sanction to Settlement: Many activities in government and enterprise domains need approvals and endorsement. Blockchain can track the documentation and attestations from approval to settlement in an impeccable manner. House designs, police approvals for public meetings, large project budgets, are some of the many such activities that can benefit from the Blockchain approach. The following solution depicts a typical document management solution by leveraging Blockchain technology to eliminate fake certificates and facilitate trusted sharing of information, guaranteed by Blockchain, while protecting from malware attacks and any form of unauthorized tampering.

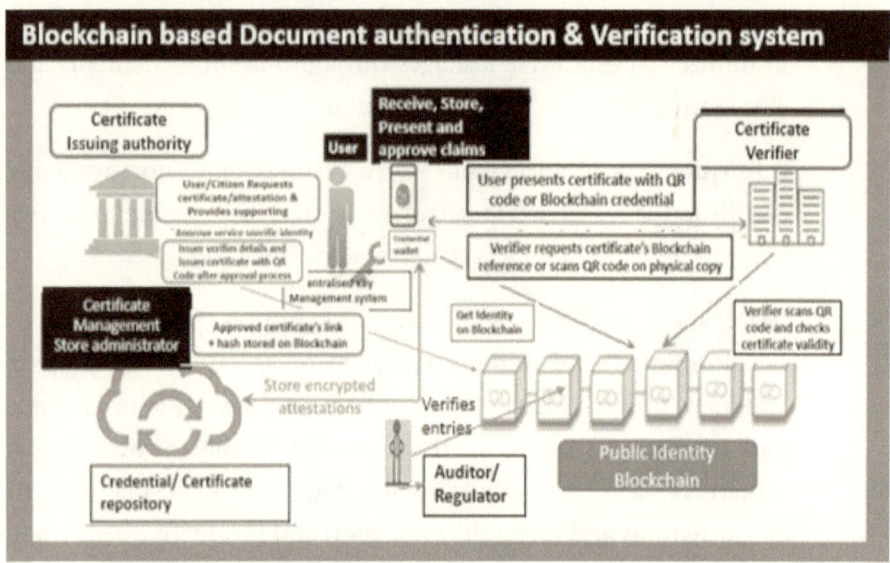

Fig 1.8 – Blockchain-based instant Document Authentication and Verification system

Loyalty programmes, games, sweepstakes and many more applications that depend on trust and relationships between hitherto unknown parties cutting across domains, will find Blockchain an interesting platform to adopt and provide value to the peers on either side. Blockchain can also help in a variety of Smart City applications to save lives and improve quality of life.

1.5 Digital Representation of Assets and Rights on a Blockchain Vide Tokenization

As we have seen earlier, the trust in the Blockchain platform which by itself is expected to act like a Disintermediating Trust machine must be above board with a due demonstration of credibility and high credentials.

For this, the consortium leading the Blockchain platform's consensus mechanism, acting as the backbone for the entire solution should comprise of many leading stalwarts in the industry who could otherwise be competitors but are acting like collaborators in the Blockchain regime. The concept of Tokenization is a powerful concept that enables real-life assets and rights to be represented as digital equivalent value units on a Blockchain. Tokenization will enable members of different peer entities (individuals or organizations) to represent their products and services in a common digital unit that can be traded. Ethereum pioneered the concept of decentralized applications that are powered by the respective Ethereum (native cryptocurrency of Ethereum Public Blockchain) compatible tokens which can be freely traded on the network. This will enable the launch of decentralized versions of all the real-life applications as we know – like Amazon, Facebook – powered by a Blockchain-based token.

LIBRA coin powered by a Blockchain platform spearheaded by Facebook, is a precursor of things to come with respect to migration of today's centralized systems onto a Blockchain-based infrastructure. Blockchain platform-based applications like LIBRA (promoted by a group with Facebook as the leading member), Hashgraph, are combining ranks of leading players in the global business ecosystem and Fortune 100 members to form strong governing boards that can act like a 'Trusted Third Party' in a foolproof manner. LIBRA is a Permissioned Blockchain digital currency proposed by the American social media company, Facebook. The project, currency and transactions are to be managed and cryptographically entrusted to the LIBRA Association – a membership of companies from payment, technology, telecommunication, online marketplace and venture capital, and nonprofits (Wikipedia).

Comparison between Centralised & Decentralised Asset coins		
Type of value exchange unit	Centralised Banking & Marketplace systems	Blockchain based decentralised systems
National Currency	Indian Rupee	Central Bank Digital Currency over a DLT
Global Currency	US Dollar	Bitcoin
Marketplace Token	Amazon Paybalance	LIBRA coin
Closed loop Merchant token	Mall Food court cash card	DAPP Token

Fig 1.9 – Understanding LIBRA coin and Bitcoin with analogies

Currently, the US Dollar is seen as the globally interoperable currency accepted by most nations. In the recent past, several countries began experimenting with the concept of leveraging the internet for speedy transfer of value, considering the impending proliferation of IoT and Industrial IoT-led home automation, industrial automation, and Smart City projects across the world. There has been a strong need for a digital equivalent of national currencies, giving rise to the concept of Central Bank Digital Currency (CBDC), also called digital fiat currency (a currency established as money by government regulation or law). CBDC is different from virtual currency and cryptocurrency, which are not issued by the state and lack the legal tender status declared by the government. Various countries are already experimenting with the concept of CBDC and it is considered a transitory step to the ultimate eventuality of a fully digitized currency with the added security measure offered by a Blockchain approach. According to the BIS, today nearly 70% of central banks are looking at CBDC, with most of them considering Blockchain as the underlying technology.

1.6 Blockchain – A Key Catalyst for Secured Automation and a World of Trusted Transactions

Recently the world witnessed the uproar raised due to the failure on the part of Facebook to protect of identities of its members in the Cambridge

Analytica case. In such a scenario, what are the alternatives for global corporate citizens to express themselves freely and be connected across the world without security breaches?

But then, there is hope. The onset of Artificial Intelligence empowered mammoth organizations with unlimited power, but the threats of cyber warfare, Ransomware and unscrupulous promoters have led to the people embracing Blockchain as a religion across the world. Blockchain has now given an unprecedented option for all peers across the world to be connected in a pseudonymous manner.

This is now leading to a movement that is going to gain strength in the future as the Blockchain paradigm cuts across the various sections of the world with a versatile, empowered, and ubiquitous ecosystem. Conventional social media will no more be the preferred choice of communication. The implementation of Blockchain-enabled KYC (Know Your Customer) and self-sovereign identity will empower citizens across the world to own their own data and use the various platforms designed for specific purposes, in a safe and secure way, while monetizing their activities.

The data in the Blockchain-enabled future will put power back into the hands of the individuals. The identities of the world's citizens will be protected by Blockchain as they operate in a pseudonymous manner with metadata visible to the advertisers and platforms. They can give permission to the platforms and data consumers, while they get paid for the same as well as for their social media contributions.

Several Blockchain-enabled platforms are already catching on and the same are listed in the book 'Blockchain – The Untold Story', which examines Blockchain technology in all earnest, for the benefit of a safe and secure future for global citizens.

Blockchain: A New World Paradigm

Welcome to a world of hope and empowerment facilitated by this amazing paradigm of our era, Blockchain. The excitement to adopt this new paradigm can be visualized by the amount of activity that is taking place across the world from companies, consortiums and countries, including the European Union and the United Nations.

Leading countries working on Blockchain use the principle "Trust, but verify" a rhyming Russian proverb, used by Former USA President Ronald Reagan in the context of nuclear disarmament discussions with the Soviet Union. Blockchain with its ability to act as a Trust Anchor and provide an auditable track record closely symbolizes this mantra. Many governments across the world are exploring/leveraging Blockchain to offer transparent, efficient and cost-effective services to their citizens and industry. The following are some of the noted efforts by governments across the world.

1. **Brazil** is using Blockchain-based Government e-Procurement to put a check on corruption in all government purchases. Online Bid Solution, a Blockchain-based platform tracks the process of public bidding for government projects and purchase processes between various cooperative societies and industry bodies.

2. **China** is leveraging Blockchain to fight corruption and disintermediate tax collections. The Chinese government is launching its own digital currency powered by Permissioned DLT (distributed ledger technology) and facilitates the Public Blockchain ecosystem in a big way. Leading companies like Alibaba, Tencent and thousands of other companies are working on implementing Blockchain projects across every possible use case, spurring innovation and efficiency to a new plane.

3. **Dubai** is patronizing Blockchain to eliminate all paper records across its governance, land records management, police evidence tracking, passport and visa tracking, cross/border remittances, citizen medical records tracking, etc., and saves 5.5 billion dirhams annually in document processing alone, equal to the worth of one Burj Khalifa every year. A sample copy of a land title deed digitized on Blockchain:

Title Deed

Issue Date	11/12/2018	تاريخ الإصدار
Mortgage Status:	Not mortgaged غير مرهونة	حالة الرهن:
Property Type:	Villa فيلا	نوع العقار:
Community:	Al Yelayiss 2 2 البلايس	المنطقة:
Plot No:	178	رقم الأرض:
Building No:	TS HYT TH-V-451	رقم المبنى:
Area Sq Meter :	196.28	المساحة الكلية متر مربع :
Area Sq Feet :	2,112.74	المساحة الكلية بالقدم المربع :

Owners numbers and their shares:	Area (Sq Meter) \ المساحة بالمتر المربع	أرقام و أسماء الملاك و حصصهم:
(5120709) RASHED AHMAD RASHED ALMULLA ALFALASI	196.28	(5120709) رائد أحمد راشد الملا الفلاسي

Purchased from NSHAMA PROPERTIES OWNED BY NSHMI DEVELOPMENT ONE PERSON COMPANY L.L.C by the Land Registration No. : 225832/2015 Date 12/11/2018 for the amount 1226888 Dirham One Million and Two Hundred and Twenty Six Thousand and Eight Hundred and Eighty Eight Dirhams Only Dirhams

أنت بالشراء من نشاما للعقارات لمالكها نشمي ديفلوبمنت شركة الشخص الواحد ش.ذ.م.م بموجب العقار رقم ٢٢٥٨٣٢/٢٠١٥ بتاريخ ١٢/١١/٢٠١٨ بمبلغ وقدره ١٢٢٦٨٨٨ درهم مليون و مئتين و ستة و عشرون ألفا و ثمانمائة و ثمانية و ثمانون درهماً فقط لا غير

This property and its ownership is subject to the terms of the jointly owned property declaration of the above mentioned community and to the regulations issued in accordance with it as may be amended from time to time

بخضع هذا العقار وملكيته لأحكام إعلان المجمع السكني للمنطقة المذكورة أعلاه، وللقواعد والتعليمات المتعلقة بذلك والتي يتم إصدارها أو تعديلها من وقت لآخر

المساحة الإجمالية المساحة طبقاً لخط التطوير () قدم مربع

Approved Signature نوقيع مصدق

43266/2018

DUBAI LAND DEPARTMENT (565) دائرة الأراضي والأملاك

- Digital data of this certificate is securely stored on blockchain
- This certificate is electronically issued and no signature is required
- Any changes in the certificate make it void
- It is prohibited to hold this certificate by any other party

1 / 1

Fig 1.10 – Blockchain record of a land title deed in Dubai

Further, Dubai is one of the leading exponents of all emerging technologies. Setting itself an ambitious target of becoming a paperless country, the Dubai Government has been pioneering Blockchain and emerging technologies through a series of measures.

4. **Estonia**, a small country with 1.3 million population and an erstwhile part of Soviet Union, is extensively using Blockchain for the integrity of data pertaining to all public and citizen records, Critical Infrastructure Protection and for secured access to all government services by citizens – through a Blockchain-enabled digital identity. Estonia secured all its citizens' medical records on a Blockchain.

5. **European Union**: European Blockchain Services Infrastructure (EBSI), launched by the European Union, enables users to store and transmit data in a secure, decentralized manner and deliver better services to European citizens.

6. **India's** Telecom Regulatory Authority is using DLT for tracking Unsolicited Commercial Communication. Several states, ministries, income tax department, customs department, Public Sector Undertakings and police departments are vigorously exploring Blockchain to improve transparency, efficiency and eliminate corruption and the fake products, documents, identity, and certificates menace.

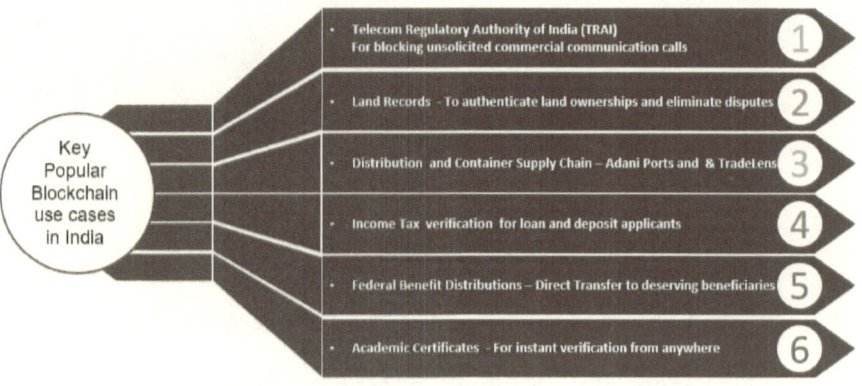

Fig 1.11 – Key popular Blockchain use cases in India

7. **Singapore** is working on a Blockchain-based payment system using digital Singapore Dollars, that can be used to execute inter-

bank and cross currency remittances quickly, affordably and with fewer intermediaries. Singapore, being a global hub for finance and supply chain activities, has prompted the Singapore government to enable a vibrant Blockchain ecosystem for enterprises to experiment and implement the entire spectrum of Permissioned and Permissionless Blockchain applications across finance, supply chain, trade finance, crowdfunding, health insurance, digital SGD, academic certificates, etc. Singapore is also building a public digital platform and an operating system to which all the public agencies are connected through a secure, sensor network providing anonymized data collected across various facets of their services to citizens. Potential applications of Blockchain Technology for Smart Cities include waste management, home automation, vehicle traffic management, land tilting and record management, P2P renewable energy metering and trading, etc.

8. **Uganda** is leveraging Blockchain in its pharma supply chain to fight fake drug menace by eliminating them.

9. The **UK** government has been exploring Blockchain for several use cases like CBDC for instant inter-bank remittances, clearing and settlement, land records management, government data provenance, voting, benefits and charity distribution and food safety in supply chains.

10. **United States**: The US government is working extensively on several Blockchain projects in pharmaceuticals, food, cannabis, defence supply chain provenance, health record tracking, clinical records management, etc. The Department of Homeland Security is researching Blockchain extensively for critical infrastructure protection using Blockchain-enabled identification systems.

11. **Thailand**: Thailand Government is extensively experimenting with Blockchain for a variety of applications involving digital identity, supply chain and Central Bank Digital Currencies.

The continuing emergence of Blockchain Consortiums in the recent past is further driving the acceptance and implementation of Blockchain-based solutions in business across the globe. Joining a consortium to study and explore Blockchain technology is very different from aggressively moving to build and deploy the technology on a significant scale. Not all consortiums will result in commercial deployments and that is perfectly fine for those participants who are more interested in learning at this point. However, enterprises with serious commercial intent may want to take it a step further and critically evaluate various facets of the Blockchain Consortium they want to join. In the subsequent chapters, we discuss the diverse attributes of the consortium such as funding, membership, leadership, and governance in detail.

Blockchain Consortium

2.1 What is Meant by 'Consortium' in General?

A consortium is a group made up of two or more individuals, companies, or governments that work together to achieve a common objective. The common objective benefits all the included parties. Examples include lobbying for regulatory changes, bidding on a large project, or increasing partners' purchasing power to get better deals. If the relationship between parties needs to be satisfactory, then it requires:

- a shared vision

- good communication

- sound policies and procedures

- effective financial, risk and environmental management systems

- a clear understanding of the practical details including potential risks; and

- access to regularly updated relevant legislation

A consortium is more than a loose partnership of organizations working and learning together (although they will do both in a consortium). It is a formal arrangement between organizations working together towards a defined objective and, of course, clarity of purpose is a very essential ingredient in the formation of a consortium. Here are some examples of consortiums in different industries:

Travel: Virtuoso (https://www.virtuoso.com/)

Virtuoso is a network of luxury travel agencies, with more than 20,000 travel advisors across the globe. It also includes 2,000 preferred suppliers, such as cruise lines, hotels, and tour operators. Together, they work for a common goal: providing exclusive travel experiences for consumers.

Education: Consortium for Global Education (CGE) (https://www. cgedu.org)

The CGE is a non-profit global organization with a membership of accredited American private universities and colleges, with consortium member campuses, located in more than 23 USA states and six nations, who are equally committed to quality programs of international education. Affiliate members represent key national universities worldwide. Each member of the consortium is committed to high value, quality academic education and supports the internationalization of higher education through student and faculty global participation.

Web Standards: World Wide Web Consortium (https://www.w3.org/)

The World Wide Web Consortium (W3C) is an international community where member organizations, a full-time staff, and the public, work together to develop Web standards. The World Wide Web Consortium (W3C) was founded in 1994 at the Massachusetts Institute of Technology Laboratory for Computer Science (MIT/LCS), with support from the European Commission and the Defence Advanced Research Projects Agency (DARPA). The organization tries to foster compatibility and agreement among industry members in the adoption of new standards defined by the W3C. The consortium tries to get all the vendors to implement a set of core principles and components which are chosen by the consortium.

2.2 Blockchain Consortium Overview

Across all the industry verticals, one common approach to Blockchain exploration and adoption that has emerged, and will probably accelerate post COVID 19, is to form a consortium with multiple stakeholders, to create, deploy and scale industry-wide solutions. The consortium model allows companies to take advantage of Blockchain technology by balancing the benefits while also protecting their competitive advantage individually, and keeping sensitive data confidential. Also, as global organizations become more competitive today for a variety of factors, the concept of coopetition has also taken centre stage. Today consortiums is one of the most prominent methods and also a preferred vehicle that organizations are using to organize collaboration and create network effects while exploring enterprise grade Blockchain solutions.

Blockchain Consortium or federated Blockchain is a type of Blockchain network where multiple organizations maintain the system. However, it's permissioned and not public. You will find it more similar to private networks. But the main twist is that even though it's permissioned, it can actually offer a decentralized structure.

How? Well, as you already know, instead of only one organization, multiple organizations take part in a consortium. As a result, every organization gets similar treatment with no single entity ruling over the network. In reality, you can think of it as a platform where multiple companies come together and share their information if needed. It's a collaborative environment, which is highly beneficial.

As the technology continues to evolve, the consortium approach can take Research and Development (R&D) to the next level, beyond what any enterprise may be able to achieve alone, to develop new Blockchain solutions for several use cases. The consortium will evolve as solutions are deployed to encourage adoption, create standards, and interoperate with other business organizations and additional consortiums.

Today, almost every industry vertical is exploring Blockchain technology either through standalone pilot projects or through a consortium. As of June 2020, they are approximately 190+ active Blockchain Consortiums operating in the market at various stages of evolution. Financial and Banking Services are leading the race in the Blockchain Consortium market.

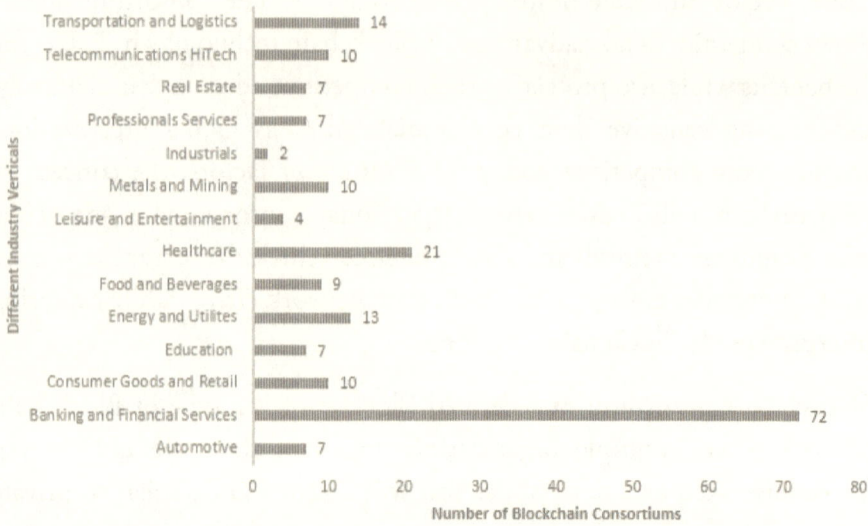

Fig 2.1 – Industry wise – Number of Blockchain Consortiums –
Source : ESG-Intelligence

2.3 Why Consortiums Are Critical for Blockchain Technology?

Consortiums have become a popular means for enterprises to work together on Blockchain technology. More than ever, many organizations have started seeing the consortium model as a viable framework for addressing the challenges associated with the implementation of Blockchain technology on a significant scale. For some organizations, consortiummodels represent a very

> The core benefits of Blockchain Technology are realized through collaborating with other parties in an ecosystem and establishing a consortia
>
> Deloitte Report

low risk entry and minimum effort to stay up-to-date with the emerging trends in Blockchain space, learn what the competitors are doing, defend against potential new threats and, most importantly, prepare a roadmap for implementation if they decide to. Some industry experts are of the view that many enterprises are joining consortiums for FOMO: fear of missing out. The new digital world will only add fuel to this FOMO hysteria as there will be an increasing trend of forced acceleration in embracing digital transformation initiatives by enterprises, just to ensure that businesses will have the ability to deliver essential functions in the world after the pandemic. In such a scenario, the Blockchain Consortium model can provide safe passage for enterprises to plan for responsible Blockchain deployment, de-risk early adoption, and ensure careful consideration of unintended consequences.

Consortiums will also play a central role in the commercialization of Blockchain technology in every industry. A consortium allows individual companies to better leverage these network effects for their own specific needs by providing them the ability to streamline business processes of common concern to all consortium members.

Distributed ledgers are business-to-business workflow tools, which entails that Blockchain practically demands collaboration—to set standards, develop infrastructure, and execute transactions for businesses. It derives more utility from network effects: The greater the number of users, the more valuable the technology is to all of them. Consortiums allow companies to take advantage of Blockchain network effects from day one, by providing a vehicle to create a governance structure around this collaboration, often among players that compete against one other. Consequently, in order to use Blockchain effectively, most enterprises need to be part of a consortium.

Data and information are the foundation upon which businesses make key decisions about everything from product development to manufacturing and marketing, and on which they create their own unique marketplace identities. Why then should any business work directly with its competitors on something as important and as potentially game-changing as Blockchain? The answer can be found in the nature and the core of the technology itself. Blockchain relies upon the decentralized nature of decision making which can significantly reduce or overcome frictions and failures inherent in the decision making processes, when different stakeholders work together for a common vision.

2.4 Benefits from Blockchain Consortiums

> Blockchain-based collaboration cannot come from a single company. Industry collaboration has to proactively drive disruption, innovation, and transformation throughout the industry by identifying and modeling areas where distributed autonomous software agents can transact on behalf of people, businesses, and things.
>
> Henrik Hvid Jensen, Senior Blockchain Adviser, Trustworks

The Blockchain Consortium model is an especially useful way for competitors to organize themselves when approaching emerging decentralized software solutions, as collaboration is needed to take advantage of the true benefits that Blockchain technology has to offer. Joining such a Blockchain Consortium could bring enterprises a number of interesting benefits, including cost savings, shared (and lower) risks, building critical mass of adoption, and offer influencing standards. Some of the key expected benefits of joining a Blockchain Consortium are:

- **Economical gains**: By the very nature of Blockchain technology, removing intermediaries can result in significant cost reductions and elimination of costly reconciliation processes for enterprises. The whole idea of being a consortium member is to avoid major capex expenses in exploring Blockchain technology for business operations, and get access to industry's best practices knowledge as well. It also allows members of the consortium to take economies of scale to the next level through co-creation – a concept that brings different parties together (e.g., a company and a group of customers) to jointly produce a mutually valued outcome in a trusted environment. So joining a consortium should offer the most cost-saving features for your industry.

- **Expedited Learning**: To grow in the Blockchain niche, you will need full support in learning. Many consortiums offer training and other development support from experts. Opportunities like that can really nurture your organization's internal capabilities and equip your team members with practical knowledge of Blockchain as well.

- **Risk Sharing:** Enterprises will definitely want a platform where every single company shares the risk in case of a new Blockchain solution. As Blockchain is still relatively new, there are a lot of risks and challenges associated with it in the marketplace for its adoption. But if members collaborate, then the overall risk is much lower whether the solutions fail or succeed.

- **Build Critical Mass of Adoption**: Critical mass for a technology is the point where it becomes self-sustaining and continues to be profitable over time. Taking the solution on a mass adoption level would help enterprises reach a new height easily. Without mass adoption, reaching the global marketplace will become tough.

- **Maintaining Lifespan**: A consortium needs to offer a relevant solution or a roadmap. It is now imperative for enterprises to keep pace with rapidly evolving technology to stay relevant or competitive in the field. Thus, as time goes on, you should expect your consortium to pivot their plans accordingly.

- **Driving Standardization:** A good consortium is expected to offer influencing standards. According to market research by leading firms, Blockchain will soon reach interoperability. And so, there will be an increasing demand for the need of influencing standards to mark the organization's place in a competitive industry.

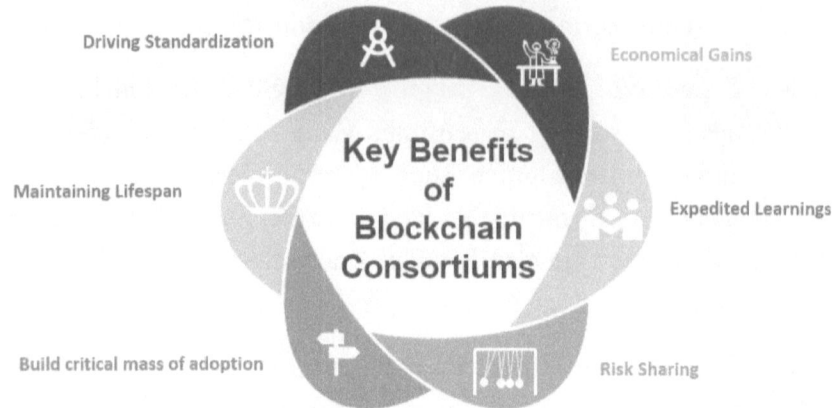

Fig 2.2 – Key Benefits of Blockchain Consortiums

2.5 Roles in Blockchain Consortium

Whenever an enterprise joins a Blockchain Consortium, the first thing they should be clear on is in what capacity they are joining in. For a Blockchain Consortium to succeed, each participant in the ecosystem will need to contribute data and resources that are beneficial to the others. Therefore, it is extremely important to define each participant's role and responsibilities when preparing for the Blockchain Consortium, and also define how participants will communicate with each other from a business perspective. Below are the typical roles followed in most of the active consortiums today:

a. **Leader:** Leadership in the consortium is always driven by the steering committee which comprises C-Suite representatives and visible champions for the consortium.

b. **Core Groups:** The core groups of the Blockchain Consortium are made up of business/technical committees/system integrators (solution providers) where the nominated points of contact from each consortium member represent their individual organization.

c. **Members (Active Participants)**: These members are responsible for project management and delivery, which includes taking responsibility for the day-to-day overseeing of individual work streams to stay on-time, on-budget, and meet quality standards. This can be undertaken by either a dedicated consortium member or employees of a consortium entity.

d. **Users**: These are the business/operational users who will be actually working on the product/platform created through the joint efforts of the consortium members.

e. **Third Party Service Providers**: They provide support services and guidance to various aspects of the operating model. They can be dedicated consortium members, or employees of a consortium entity or a third-party network operator.

Leader/s	Core group	Members or active participants	Users	Third party service provider/s
These are the organisation/s with the vision for the network and its business benefits. Typically, the originator/s of the project and the primary benefactor/s of the work	This will be a group of leading or Active Organizations who crystallize the operational activities or actively manage the ecosystem	The group of primary participants in the network that contribute governance, data, and workflow	Participants that derive benefits from the network and can access their own data but are not responsible for actively managing the network	Third parties offering services to the network which may include infrastructure, applications, IT support services and other services typically for a fee

Participants will at least need to take one of
the roles. However, in most cases, they would
assume more than one role

Fig 2.3 – Typical Roles in a Blockchain Consortium
Source: World Economic Forum

Blockchain Consortiums – Different Flavours

3.1 Overview of Different Flavours

Every enterprise has different business goals, risk tolerance and risk appetite. For that reason, not all consortiums are created equal, nor are they designed to achieve the same goals for their members. Today, there are a variety of consortium types and models that provide differing levels of access and serve specific needs. Determining the type of consortium the organization wants to join is based, in part, on what the core business activity of the organization is, and on what the organization hopes to achieve. For the purposes of our discussion, we focus on three consortium models:

1. Business Focused Consortium

    - Business process focused

    - Industry-centric focused

2. Technology Focused Consortium

3. Government-driven Consortium

Let's understand each type in detail and see some specific examples as well.

Business Focused Consortium:

Business focused consortiums primarily aim to build and operate Blockchain-based business platforms to solve a specific business problem such as

We.Trade (earlier called Digital Trade Chain), launched in January 2017 by seven leading European banks, focused on "building a Blockchain-based platform design to facilitate cross-border trade for small and medium-sized businesses"; the consortiums's members include Deutsche Bank, Société Générale, Rabobank, and UniCredit, who all agreed to collaborate and fund the development of the new platform). Other examples include BankChain, TradeLens, etc. This type of Blockchain Consortium solely focuses on a specific use case of Blockchain, such as banking, supply chain, healthcare, etc. Instead of offering open source platforms, many of them focus on commercial purposes only. They can be further categorized as Business process focused consortiums which deal with very specific business processes in a particular industry and industry-centric consortiums which aim to address industry-specific challenges such as KYC, trade finance, logistics, certifications, etc.

- **Business Process Consortium:** Business process consortiums aim to develop Blockchain solutions to reduce costs, friction, or risks involved in business activities. In the maritime industry, the Lloyd's Register has provided financing for Maritime Blockchain Labs, a consortium looking at ways to improve security in the selection of ship crews and improve crew documentation and certification. Ant Financial, Alibaba's financial services arm, in cooperation with four Australian and New Zealand food production companies, as well as with China's customs agency and logistics company, Cainiao, offers another good example of a business process-focused consortium. Food fraud has been a huge issue in China, given the country's large and growing import market. In 2008, for example, three hundred thousand infants fell ill, and six died, after drinking formula made with contaminated milk. Ant Financial has an operational Blockchain traceability solution, which has been implemented on the Tmall e-commerce platform for a variety of products, including imported milk powder and formula, honey products, organic rice, wine, and liquor, with more than 150 million traced items as of November 2018. A representative from Ant Financial stated that in October 2018 that "each traced item is issued a unique Blockchain certificate that allows consumers to look up the provenance, supply-chain, and quality assurance information through the Alipay mobile app. Small producers can also differentiate their products from lower quality copycats on the market thanks to the traceability solution."

- **Industry-centric consortium**: Some of the best-known consortiums in Blockchain are based on industry linkages. For example, the Energy Web Foundation, based in Zug, Switzerland, identifies and develops Blockchain use cases across the energy supply chain. The Blockchain Insurance Industry Initiative, originally a European project, was formed to assess Blockchain innovation in the reinsurance industry. The Mobility Open Blockchain Initiative includes members of the automotive value chain, and the Blockchain in Transportation Alliance focuses on developing standards for Blockchain use in the logistics and transport industries. Industry-based consortium are usually focused on a shared problem and they gather to address industry-specific challenges such as KYC, trade finance, logistics, certifications, and standards. In many cases, these consortiums also create an open forum for discussing these issues.

Technology Focused Consortiums:

Technology focused consortium mainly seek to develop reusable Blockchain platforms based on agreed-upon technical standards, and are often used by a variety of businesses in areas such as finance, technology, and manufacturing. Mainly these consortiums have multipurpose use cases and rally around a platform, or another technological approach, as a first principle for solution development. Two of the best-known examples of this are Hyperledger, an "open source collaborative effort created to advance cross-industry Blockchain technologies." and the Enterprise Ethereum Alliance. Both were formed with the goal of enabling interorganizational collaboration, and both promote the need for interoperability between ledgers. Members include leading companies in finance, banking, logistics, and manufacturing, such as SAP, IBM, Intel, Fujitsu, and Daimler. Moreover, this type of Blockchain industry consortium exists solely for the purpose of helping Blockchain reach global recognition. A third example for the technology-centred consortium is R3, which was born out of an initial partnership between financial service institutions and technology providers. R3 is the creator of the (now) open source Corda platform. As one of the first participants in the Hyperledger project, and because of its financial services industry affiliation, R3 enjoys a certain amount of influence. The organization has been involved in multiple high-profile proofs of concept and pilots in financial services, including a collaboration with HSBC, ING, and Cargill to capture and share trade finance Letters of Credit, as well as initiatives with the Bank of Thailand and Central Bank of Canada. Because multiparty enterprise-scale implementation has been extremely hard to achieve. However, some original R3 consortium members have lost faith and moved on.

Government-driven Consortiums:

These types of consortiums utilize a diversity of governance structures that are designed to balance public taxpayer interests with real-world challenges, while ensuring that each stakeholder has a forum to provide strategic input. The aim is to enable collaboration of an industry or multiple industries to help solve or address common regulatory challenges and facilitate the implementation of new, innovative solutions. Two out of three of the best-known examples in this category are from the Indian Blockchain space. The first is the Telecom Regulatory Authority of India (TRAI) which is a government body promoting Blockchain framework along with all leading telecom operators to curb the problem of Unsolicited Commercial Communication (UCC) or spam calls and messages, and the second is India's Income Tax Department (ITD) mandated Blockchain-based solution to improve its tax processes. Its experience envisioning and building solutions for all stakeholders provides valuable lessons to CIOs who are considering using DLT. The third and final one is from Singapore, where Monetary Authority of Singapore (MAS) partnered with a number of financial institutions and enterprise Blockchain technology companies to create Project Ubin to explore the potential of Blockchain technology.

3.2 Blockchain Consortium – Best Fit Industry Sectors

Industrial Blockchain applications have begun to emerge to improve revenue or operational performance by sharing immutable data among companies, government entities, and trade organizations. Now, it becomes clear that a consortium platform is a worthy innovation that drives the adoption of Blockchain. There are specific industries for which the consortium approach suits well, and also, those industry verticals have been early adopters in the Blockchain space.

- **Financial Services:** Blockchain innovators in financial services aren't just small startups or fintechs. Many of them are medium-sized banks and large institutions. Defying expectations, they are proving that they have the agility to move fast in the face of change. A common example from the financial services space would be regarding the issuance and trading of assets. A group of banks create a shared database where all necessary information about creditors is commonly collected and stored. Whenever a bank needs the information to identify and assess someone, the bank takes it from the distributed ledger. Another common application is KYC where the formation of the consortium lays the foundation for a nationwide, unified ecosystem for sharing of enhanced and validated KYC data. An example of a consortium here is we.trade, the trade finance network created by IBM on Hyperledger Fabric, that helps businesses create an ecosystem of trust for global trade. It empowers the participants with fully automated order-to-payment process on Smart Contracts and aims to eliminate risks of international payments and transactions. Its standardized rules and simplified trading options decrease risk and increase opportunity for banks and SMEs (small and medium-sized enterprises).

- **Supply Chain and Logistics:** Consortium is an optimal solution for creating a network for all supply chain participants. It is useful for product tracking in order to identify its provenance and the way of supplying. Most importantly, it enables true information sharing and collaboration across supply chains, thereby increasing industry innovation, reducing trade friction and, ultimately, promoting more global trade. A real-world example here is GenuineWay which is a consortium of over 500 authorized suppliers and distributors. The consortium applies QR codes to food and liquor items. Finally, Smart Contracts are deployed to certify the manufacturer of artisanal food products for end consumers.

- **Healthcare and Insurance:** The cost-effectiveness of Blockchain solutions in healthcare depends on a number of factors, including the use case applied, the size and demographics of the implementing organizations, and the requirements of the consortium or governance model. Adoption may impact both, potential costs and savings. Every time a person visits a hospital, he/she claims insurance payment. In order to speed up this process, hospitals and insurance companies may join the consortium to exchange information and money seamlessly, and without paperwork. Furthermore, this will enable insurers to reduce the risk of data breaches, fraud and money laundering, while delivering a superior experience to customers through improved process efficiency, better record-keeping, and accelerated turnaround time. A good example of this is the Synaptic Health Alliance consortium (**https://www.synaptichealthalliance.com**) formed by Aetna, Cognizant, Humana, MultiPlan, Optum, Quest Diagnostics and UnitedHealthcare. The goal of this consortium is to tackle the challenge of accurate and efficient provider data management and sharing, among the partner entities. The current regulation requires insurers to maintain accurate data about physicians and other providers. and hence each regulated organization ordinarily maintains a separate registry. However, that information is continuously changing, which leads insurers to invest a lot of money and effort into ensuring that the data is accurate. In April 2018, the consortium announced that they were launching a pilot program to see if Blockchain could reduce administrative costs and improve data quality. By sharing information through a distributed ledger, they are hoping to make the ecosystem more efficient.

- **Government and Public Sector**: Governments and public sector organizations leverage Blockchain technology to move away from siloed and inefficient centralized systems. Their current systems are inherently insecure and costly, while Blockchain networks offer more secure, agile, and cost-effective structures. Governments can further provide cybersecurity, process optimization, and integrate hyperconnected services while bolstering trust and accountability using Blockchain-based solutions. Given below are some examples where the government has partnered with either public or private players to help solve or address common regulatory challenges and facilitate implementation of new, innovative solutions for the benefit of the citizens.

  a. Telecom Regulatory Authority of India (TRAI) – a government agency in India along with Tech Mahindra, a leading provider of digital transformation and consulting and Microsoft, formed a partnership to create a DLT-based solution for mitigating the issue of UCC which is a major nuisance to telecom subscribers across the country. The DLT-based solution brings all the relevant parties in the ecosystem onto Blockchain, helping telecom service providers and telemarketers take care of preference registration, consent acquisition, dynamic preference setting, stakeholder onboarding, header registration, template registration, scrubbing service, and complaint handling and tracking – which are in line with the tenets of the TRAI regulation. The solution will be a shared, secured ledger of UCCs distributed across a network of computers, which will ensure a transparent and verifiable system to help companies mitigate UCC on their networks. It conforms to the recently passed TRAI regulation and will enable all ecosystem players to comply with it.

b. Income Tax Department of India along with their technology partner Infosys decided to address the broader tax ecosystem concerns which include banks, financial institutions, government agencies, enterprises, and individuals by creating a trust-based institutional collaboration where multiple entities share data securely and concurrently, without a lot of point-to-point connections, through a Permissioned Blockchain-based solution.

c. Project Ubin that started in 2016, a collaborative project driven by the MAS is a consortium effort that explores the benefits of DLT on implementing a real-time gross settlement solution in central banking. The project aims to help MAS and the industry better understand the technology and the potential benefits it may bring through practical experimentation. This is with the eventual goal of developing simpler to use and more efficient alternatives to today's systems based on central bank issued digital tokens. Project Ubin is a multi-year multi-phase project, with each phase aimed at solving the pressing challenges faced by the financial industry and the Blockchain ecosystem. We believe that eventually this approach will become the global benchmark for governments across the globe to experiment with technologies such as Blockchain that aim to increase transparency and heighten efficiencies. Please refer to the annexure for more details on Project Ubin's use cases.

3.3 Blockchain Consortium Business Models

With Blockchain Consortium enabled solutions, enterprises can turn their businesses into decentralization platforms which can alter how their businesses works. It changes the individual elements, the flow of transactions, profits, and also ensures growth. However, to succeed properly, Blockchain Consortium business models should make sure that they benefit all member participants equally. A Blockchain Consortium's business model's key considerations include the following:

- Cost optimization and Systemic Risk mitigation

- Avenues for new business growth due to co-creation of elements

- Competition versus cooperation

The most commonly used Blockchain Consortium business models can be broadly classified into three categories:

a. Traditional Utility Token Business Model

b. Not-for-Profit Blockchain Business Model

c. For-Profit Blockchain Business Model

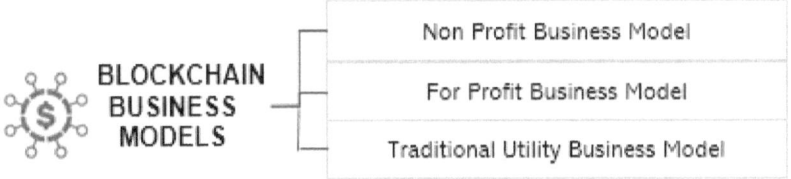

Fig 3.1 – Different types of Blockchain business models

- **Traditional Utility Token Business Model:**

  The utility token model drives functionality in business via the use of the tokens. Ripple and Stellar are great examples of these kinds of models. The banks who are part of their network can facilitate fund transfer via the use of the XRP or XLM tokens. Token utility model is a Blockchain traditional business model that can encourage broad market participation, while also providing initial investors with a means for creating and recouping value around a new platform. Under this model, a consortium first offers basic functionality such as network consensus, dissemination and verification of transactions, basic models for Smart Contracts, tokenized properties, or digital documents as a kind of utility. User fees are based on a cost-driven model and any surplus profits are allocated to all market participants based on some measure of use, such as volume or value channelled through the platform. Intellectual property (IP) rights are retained by the initial investors, participants, or the platform's creators.

The other two most popular business models for Blockchain-led consortium projects are:

- **For-Profit Business Model:**

The pure for-profit model is used where the private sector drives growth and there is the possibility of an extraordinary medium-term value as seen in other supply chain projects. Many Blockchain Consortiums today follow this model. Essentially, the actual corporate structure may be spun out as a JV, as in the case of the eight banks that formed Contour, or they can have a hybrid business model in which only a few participants support IP and others lease the technology out. Such forms of spin-outs arise well after the initial pre-consortium formation steps are taken.

The problems of antitrust are a persistent concern for Blockchain Consortiums. Excessive caution should be taken in the for-profit scenario about potential monopoly allegations and strict oversight and enforcement of checks against collusive behaviour. Permit to regulate should be obtained where appropriate. For example, the Federal Maritime Commission recently granted an antitrust exemption to TradeLens, a Blockchain shipping consortium originally formed by IBM and Maersk GTD, so that the five major container line shipping companies involved can collaborate efficiently in the provision of data for use on the platform.

- **Not-for-profit Business Model:**

The not-for-profit Blockchain business model is generally based on a particular industry challenge that has substantial social effects. Such groups may act as open source projects and also may have participation from the public or private sectors. Increasingly, many companies which intend to join the Blockchain Consortium are choosing this non-profit business models to defend against future antitrust concerns. In the case of RiskStream (now RiskBlock), a Blockchain Consortium in the insurance industry organized itself as a non-profit to create a platform that will be useful to insurance industry players. Consortiums using this model should employ a two-tier approach: build the underlying structure as a non-profit such as RiskBlock or create a for-profit ecosystem that sits on top of the platform. Alternatively, a for-profit organization might create the platform first and then hand it over to a non-profit – perhaps a foundation or similar agency – that will run the platform afterwards.

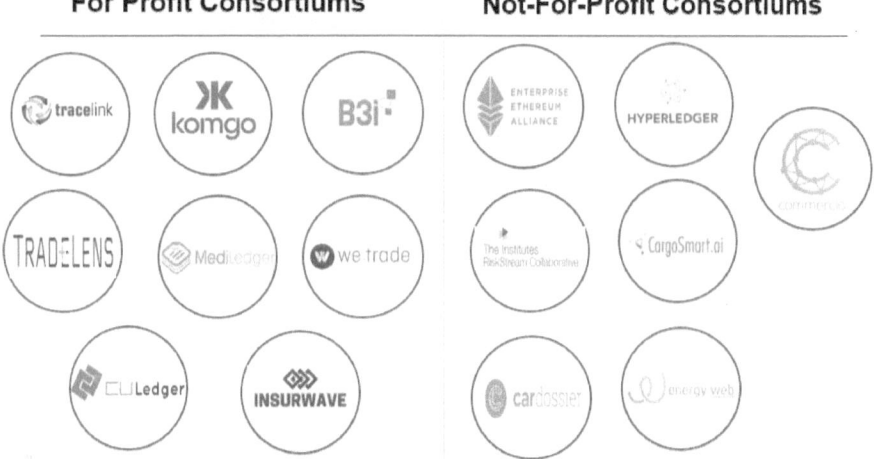

Fig 3.2 – Examples of Consortiums Organized by For-profit Versus Not-for-profit (As of January 2020)

Consortium Formation

4.1 Overview

As the Blockchain technology separates itself from the cryptocurrency frenzy, enterprises around the world are trying to find effective, viable, scalable, and sustainable use cases of this technology. As Steve Jobs put it aptly a few years ago – "***Great things in business are never done by one person. They're done by a team of people.***" If we take this quote and apply it in the context of Blockchain technology, it would read something like – "***Great things on the Blockchain are never done by one organization. They're done by a consortium of organizations***". Today, Blockchain technology has several strong use cases in each industry but requires collaboration among industry stakeholders to test, pilot and commercialize these Blockchain applications. Among different industry verticals, one common approach to Blockchain exploration and adoption that has emerged is to form a consortium among multiple stakeholders with the intent to create, deploy, accelerate, and scale industry-wide solutions. The Blockchain Consortium model allows participants to take advantage of Blockchain technology by balancing the benefits, which often include allowing competitors to collaborate to create decentralized network solutions to solve shared problems, while also protecting their competitive advantages individually and keeping sensitive data confidential. Gartner predicts that by 2023, 10% of all large organizations will join a Blockchain Consortium with the specific purpose of improving their level of customer service.

As this nascent Blockchain technology continues to emerge, the consortium approach can take R&D to the next level, beyond what an enterprise may be able to achieve alone, to develop new Blockchain solutions that address specific supply-chain use cases. The consortium can evolve as the solutions are deployed to encourage adoption, create standards, and interoperate with other business organizations and additional consortiums. For example, a proof of concept (POC) may start out in-house at a single company or with a small group of participants within an industry, then, grow over time in terms of vertical and horizontal participation, technical sophistication, or both.

The journey to create a multi-company Blockchain Consortium can be inherently awkward as making sudden big bang changes to decades-old enterprise methodologies is certainly a Herculean task to achieve under any circumstances. The consortium arrangement often forms organically with a few companies or among participants within a single company who are interested in exploring Blockchain technology further. They may start out with a POC in-house or with a small group of participants within an industry or across a market vertical.

When such experiments succeed and begin to grow in usage, it may be necessary to work more formally with other industry competitors, suppliers, and participants to enable interoperability, set more stringent data and protocol standards, and to ensure industry-wide adoption. Going forward, Blockchain Consortiums will play a major role in Blockchain adoption and these Blockchain Consortiums take many forms. While some enterprises align and collaborate in a genuine collective model to pursue common goals, others represent the vision of a single, powerful entity exerting influence over industry subordinates. In order to increase the probability of success of the consortium at an early stage, and also to maximize the consortium's opportunities, a very careful and holistic approach is required. The size of a consortium can grow quickly, and without a proper structure in place, it will be a mammoth task to manage the interests of all the stakeholders in a democratic way. A classic example of this is the R3 consortium which started in September 2015 with nine banks and has since evolved and grown. By December 2015 there were 42 members. Such rapid growth can destabilize a consortium if the right rules that allow for the growth and evolution of the group are not in place from the beginning. Setting best practices for the consortium at the outset is critical. With the right structures in place, a consortium can thrive and build on its successes. There are several key questions that key decision makers of the organizations should consider before determining which type of consortium, new or existing, is right for the organization. These questions include the following:

Fig 4.1 – Key Questions for Decision Makers

4.2 Nailing the Pre-consortium Agreement – Key Considerations

A consortium does not form out of thin air. Usually a few industry players get together in a working group to explore Blockchain technology within and across an industry. This working group can be regarded as a "seed group" that precedes the formation of a formal consortium. Not all working groups lead to consortium formation. But those who do, can benefit from having a pre-consortium agreement in existence as a roadmap. Pre-consortium agreements, by contrast, are more flexible than consortium agreements, and are created for the short term or for a very limited purpose. They are negotiated relatively quickly, and they tend to support a single use case or short-duration research and exploration. Thus, entities seeking to build use cases or test concepts often enter into pre-consortium agreements to set expectations, distribute responsibilities, and manage IP. The pre-consortium agreement can represent the 'toe in the water' approach to working with others as a group heads toward forming a formal consortium.

To mitigate any negative impact and plan for future viability with this nascent technology, it is imperative that decision makers are aware of misconceptions that can lead to disappointment and failure in Blockchain Consortium initiatives. To avoid any kind of pitfalls, a pre-consortium agreement is generally a starting step which is used to define the expectations that all involved parties bring to the table. A good analogy here is to think of couples who are planning a marriage. But before marriage, the couples get engaged and the most important reason a couple gets engaged has traditionally been to prepare them for marriage. An engagement changes the status of a couple and demonstrates their commitment not just to each other, but also to a change of lifestyle. Similarly when enterprises want to enter into formal partnerships or joint ventures with their suppliers and competitors, they first get engaged which, in this context, is through the pre-consortium agreement. When all the key considerations are properly evaluated, the pre-consortium agreement can act as a road test for participants to see how they might work together in a more formal relationship in the future. At the outset, four major challenges must be met which can collectively be referred to as the code of practice. They include:

a. Agreement on the set-up of the new entity

b. Enumeration of shared goals and key success factors

c. Operating rules and responsibilities

d. Memorandum of Understanding (MOU) committing the agreement to writing

4.2.1 Define the New Entity's Business Case and Operating Structure

Blockchain technology, while evolving rapidly, is still not proven to completely satisfy enterprise needs. It is important for the participants of the consortium to brainstorm collectively, using design-thinking workshops for use cases, business justification, viability and sustainable use cases. These workshops generally help participants get a detailed business Value Proposition with potential return on investment (ROI) suggested. Consortium members should be provided with information outlining the minimum number of members required to establish a viable ecosystem to support and drive future success. A Blockchain Consortium usually involves complex relationships among established industry players working alongside competitors. In the midst of these complicated relationships, they are all trying to understand, explore, and create industry solutions using an emerging technology which, while increasingly understood, has not yet had its value proven at scale. Hence it's essential to set realistic expectations upfront, as consortiums always benefit from early alignment and buy-in among potential members while setting the agreements. With that in mind, a consortium agreement can provide stability as it spells out formal and detailed rules and responsibilities for the long-term sustainability of the consortium.

4.2.2 Define Shared Goals and Key Success Factors

Despite the fact that the technology is still in a nascent stage of its development and adoption, as it continues to evolve, it is important for all the participants to understand the functional definition of the entire suite of Blockchain, or DLT, along with legal and regulatory issues and other implementation prerequisites. Equally important is the fact that this technology may not be universally more efficient and thus specific use cases need to be identified where it adds value and those where it does not. Hence the working group can anchor its efforts and vision on developing a POC, pilot, research report, or standards document for an initial use case whose value is universally acknowledged. This will serve as a checkpoint to test the value and success of the initial collaborative format and working group. Existing members and potential members should discuss their individual and shared goals for the consortium and establish agreement on key factors related to its purpose, vision, and definition of "success".

Also, the members may want to carefully assess their respective enterprise's risk appetite. The value in a Blockchain system can be reaped only when all the involved parties adopt it and when more of the workload transfers to the new system. Hence all the members may want to agree on a pilot use case or POC. It is important to break down the big ideas and vision of a consortium into something that can be realistically implemented.

4.2.3 Define Operating Rules and Responsibilities

Once the ground rules for the Blockchain ecosystem have been designed and the participants have come together to engage in common activities, the core objective of the working group should be to understand and explore how it will set out governing and operating rules. They must then identify and document with a clear delineation of rights and responsibilities to be distributed to teams across multiple enterprises that work toward common business goals. To be successful, however, a consortium must have a clear and equitable financial and operating model. Adequate attention should be paid to creating an agreement that does not create antitrust issues and proper plans should be discussed if regulatory permissions are required.

The ability to agree, align, and execute on key operating decisions is typically a fundamental factor for the success of any consortium. Therefore, the mechanism for how these decisions will be made, how participants will vote, and the types of decisions participants are responsible for, should be carefully considered and diligently implemented by an agile and evolving governance structure acceptable to all participants. Members should also agree on a regular meeting schedule to address issues relating to the consortium's overall performance and growth potential, and establish appropriate committees and boards to execute such governance like a Board of Directors, Advisors, Technical Steering Committees and legal committees.

4.2.4 Blueprinting the Memorandum of Understanding (MOU)

A Memorandum of Understanding (MOU or MoU) is an agreement between two or more parties outlined in a formal document. It is not legally binding but signals the willingness of the parties to move forward with a contract. When the members of the working group are not committed yet to move towards forming a consortium, but instead want to try out the group relationship in context of Blockchain activities, then the next logical step for the working group should be to consider blueprinting all the requirements and entering into a pre-consortium agreement in the form of a MOU. This agreement should be the principal guiding document with a clear allocation of rules and responsibilities for participants, as well as the role of the group itself, along with its responsibility, risk and liability. MOUs are generally very flexible and not uniform because their content is determined by the pre-consortium objectives. There are no standard forms or templates. The MOU serves multiple practical purposes, in addition to setting an initial intent for participation and understanding. Typically, the MOU addresses goals and priorities, sets out services offered, enforces mutual respect of individual and group organizational practices, provides indemnity and liability, sets out contributions, operations, governance, offers amendment/modification processes and rules for exits, and for new member admissions. Consortium development is a time-intensive and a managerially demanding activity and hence it is always a brilliant idea to establish a timeframe for turning such agreements into official participation contracts.

4.3 Consortium Formation – Key Steps

In recent years, an increasing number of Blockchain Consortiums have emerged. However, very little is known about how these consortiums were developed and what tensions emerge in such collaborations at an initial stage, what role each consortium member plays, what challenges members face in collaborating, and what aspects a digital transformation leader should consider when deciding whether to join a Blockchain Consortium. Having said that, once all the participants of the working group establish a healthy working relationship over a certain time period and intend to become a formal consortium entity, they need to review a summary of issues in priority order that must be thought through when forming a consortium. The steps for process review below are intended to serve as a useful starting point..

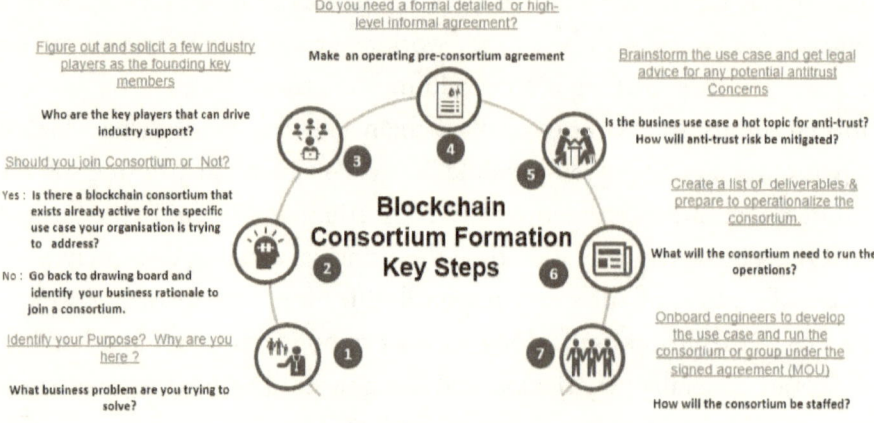

Fig 4.2 – Blockchain Consortium Formation – Key Steps

Steps	Description
Step 1 : Identify your purpose: Why are you here?	• Identify a real problem and make a sound business decision that Blockchain is appropriate technology. What business problem is one trying to solve?

Step 2 :	
Should you join a consortium or not?	• Decide whether to start a consortium or join an existing one. It is often easier and faster to leverage underlying tech than to embark on a new project. • Is there a Blockchain Consortium that exists already for the specific use case your organization is trying to address?
Step 3: Solicit leading players as the key founding members.	• Who are the key players who can drive industry support?
Step 4 : Create an operating agreement: Do you need a formal detailed or high-level informal agreement?	• Create a pre-consortium operating agreement
Step 5 : Brainstorm your enterprise use case and get legal advice for any potential antitrust concerns.	• Is the business use case a hot topic for antitrust concerns? How can the antitrust risk be mitigated?
Step 6 : Create a list of deliverables and prepare to operationalize the consortiums.	• What will the consortium need to run the operations?
Step 7 : Onboard subject matter experts and engineers to develop the use case and run the consortium or group under the signed MOU.	• How will the consortium be staffed?

Chris Ballinger (CEO and Founder of MOBI) had a set of top tips for any aspiring consortium. Run the consortium as a not-for-profit, as a for-profit consortium may arouse suspicions and members may become reluctant to join. Have full-time people working on the consortium to ensure focus. Have the members pay up their dues to support the costs of running the consortium. To do that, the consortium needs to produce a credible vision of where it's going and why it's important; how it creates a competitive advantage that is desirable in their relevant industry. Finally, ensure that there is enough expertise from within the industry, especially when it comes down to writing standards.

Managing the life cycle
of a car with blockchain technology.

A real-life interesting example to understand the ground conditions involved in the formation and evolution of a consortium is the Cardossier Blockchain Consortium in Switzerland, which is building a system to manage car data, and seeking to improve collaboration between players in the car-related ecosystem. The aim of the Cardossier consortium is to manage the lifecycle of a car and thus improve collaboration between garages, insurers, state agencies and other players in the used-car market. With this example, we wanted to highlight the core tensions involved in establishing a viable Blockchain Consortium. The consortium's goal is to build a reliable and secure "single source of truth" that removes the need to rely on a third party for data exchange and audit, and that involves various organizations from the car-related ecosystem with different interests and incentives. Initial members of the Cardossier consortium included multiple participants from the private sector (an insurance company, an importer, an official car dealer, a carsharing company and a software development partner), the public sector (Swiss Road Traffic Agency) and two research institutions. To put things in context, it would make sense to understand why the consortium was formed in the first place. Cardossier was trying to address three specific problems:

- Conflicting and unreliable data stored by different organizations in local silo databases

- Unmanageable and inefficient business processes of different enterprises

- The lack of transparency and trust between individuals and organizations

During the incorporation phase, the consortium faced several paradoxical tensions which we will examine in detail and get a glimpse of the action taken by the consortium to resolve those tensions. The primary phase of the Cardossier project covered activities such as conceptualizing the idea, preparing the project including the financial plan, and the setting up of the project. The venture commenced in November 2016 as a research/innovation initiative by AdNovum, a Swiss software company, and the University of Zurich. The collaboration started informally with idea-generation and conceptualization of the project. AdNovum and the researchers set about identifying specific use cases that might extensively benefit from trust enhancement. After considering several alternatives, the researchers finalized the used-vehicle marketplace as the most probable and relevant use case for Blockchain technology. The most significant reasons for the participants' initial hesitation were:

- too much dependency on other participating partners and lack of trust

- distorted understanding of benefits the collaboration could offer their businesses

- regulatory constraints and insufficient resources

Thus, numerous agencies from different parts of the auto-related ecosystem were invited to take part in the venture. However, possible competitors to begin with were excluded to avoid any potential conflict between them which could have endangered the mission's success.

Tension 1: Enable Trust-free Collaboration vs. Need for Interorganizational Trust

The first and foremost tension that arose in the formation phase was the need to create a system that enabled trust-free collaboration, allowing the individuals and firms to transact without the need to trust each other. The consortium participants understood that to address the lack of trusted car data throughout the lifecycle of a car, all car-related industries and agencies needed to collaborate – only then would the consortium be able to digitize all data relating to a car throughout its lifecycle. During the consortium's formative phase, when membership was restricted to just non-competing organizations, it was important to create transparent and open communication, clear information flows and consensual decision making within the consortium. The organizational structure was also established during this phase and the distribution of roles was agreed upon, along with the key organizational components – steering committee, project management team, operational team and research board.

Tension 2: Cooperation and Collaboration vs. Disintermediation

The second tension which popped up during the formative phase and also worth mentioning was the demarcation between the need to cooperate and collaborate vs the need to disintermediate. Due to this, the participants were not able to decide on what the priority was. This tension was resolved by separating the two activities: shaping and co-designing the system to achieve operational efficiencies today, and considering the potential for new business benefits when using the Cardossier platform in the future. The innovative nature of the project and awareness of the problems to be addressed by the project, fostered the successful formation of the consortium.

4.4 Checklist – Common Concerns During Pre-consortium Agreement

Given below is the list of the most common concerns a consortium might encounter in its early formative stage. Of course, every consortium or working group will have unique considerations of its own, in which case it makes sense for them to customize from this general overview. Any concerns or conflicts arising from prior working groups now transitioning toward a consortium arrangement, need to be identified and resolved when entering into pre-consortium agreements. Though not exhaustive, the list given below can act as a good starting point for formulating a pre-consortium agreement.

- Purpose and Objective of the Consortium:

  - Strategic alignment of all the participants on the business problem the consortium is aiming to address

  - Identification and decision on the key drivers of the group – Standards, Protocols, Interoperability and Regulatory

- Define Operational Strategy of the Consortium:

  - Identify initial consortium duties, roles and responsibilities of each member, including secondment rules

  - Use case development and managing anti-competitive implications, if any

  - Define the main consortium deliverables – some typical deliverables include:

    - Standard setting

    - Sharing of R&D

    - Design and develop a joint Blockchain-based platform

  - Operating Agreement – how the business is to be paid for and operated, including communication and responsibilities, both internally and externally. Also, how technology decisions including interoperability concerns are to be made (initial and ongoing choices, development, reviews, testing, changes, and updates)

- Creating staffing plans along with hiring and managing vendors and consultants

- Brand creation and marketing strategy of the pre-consortium group

- Voting structure to operate the agreement

- Committees required for the effective management of the consortium

- Data Management Governance and IP ownership

Once again, the above-mentioned checklist is just a starting point to guide enterprises or the working group through the pre-agreement phase and create a very robust structure for the consortium foundation. Also, no two consortiums are the same, so in real life there may be unique considerations for each consortium depending on the use case selection – in which case it will make sense to customize from this general overview of concerns. In the next chapter, we deal with the most important component of the consortium – the governance mechanism – and take a look at the different governance models

CHAPTER 5.0

Consortium Governance

5.1 Overview

The main success factor to get a consortium off the ground is to have collaboration-minded people at the outset who are willing to work with their peers to solve common pain points for the industry's customers. Once a real business case is identified, moving quickly to a legal entity with a profit motive will certainly help focus minds on the delivery of a product the community will pay for. Participants must keep an agile mindset and be open to change.

Bob Crozier, Head of Allianz Global Blockchain Center of Competence and B3i Board Member

Most modern organizations today, whether public or private, are highly centralized, and they typically institute bureaucratic governance that benefits monopolies. Such a centralized structure in organizations has either limited or no visibility, trust, and transparency across the business and among the partners in the value chain. These challenges drive higher costs, reduce agility and add inefficiency in operations within the organization, and can also be detrimental to the overall ecosystem of the organization, including partners, suppliers and vendors. With the emergence of Blockchain inspired solutions, there is a growing trend of centralized businesses embracing decentralization. These decentralizations can happen in two ways: centralized organizations embracing the need for institutional change can make incremental changes, or new entrants offering alternative ways such as forming a consortium to create value can make a stronger push towards decentralization. Hence, for these reasons, good governance will be a key indicator of a well-functioning consortium. Creating the sustainable framework for entities to effectively work together is just as important as building the related technology solution. Naturally, members of a consortium will have different priorities and interests that need to be reconciled. Thus, before forming a consortium, it is important to plan in advance how decisions will be made and how differences of opinions will be resolved. While there is no rule of thumb or a guidebook that will enable every distinct interest to be accommodated, establishing ground rules early can immensely help smooth disagreements or even prevent them altogether.

A hallmark of a high-performing consortium is the establishment and maintenance of a governance model that aligns the interests of all the participants involved in the Blockchain ecosystem. Streamlining important decisions such as who will fund the operations, who will be responsible for the development of the new technology and who will own the IP assets etc., is key, and a dominant factor in determining the future success of a consortium. A good governance model will include fundamental policies that enable a collaborative ecosystem and ensure that all participants are held to the highest standards – while receiving value.

5.1.1 Rethinking Traditional Governance Model

In the past, IT has always relied on conventional governance models. The traditional business governance models are generally process-heavy and require the presence of many stakeholders, intermediaries and third parties, due to limited trust and transparency. These characteristics drive inefficiencies, higher costs, and sluggishness in the business. Simply stated, for enterprises to survive and prosper they must respond to the changing competitive realities of the market. Traditional IT governance has neither the scope nor agility to meet the needs of digital business. In transitioning to a flexible governance model, which may range from a self-governance network to a consortium-defined, semi-autonomous governance structure that is fit for digital, the consortium members must act as a change agent, influencing and orchestrating the overall transformation required for the success of the consortium.

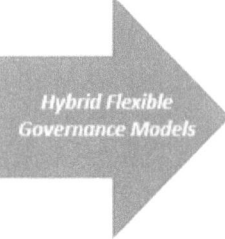

Traditional Governance Models

Disruptive Technologies
Flatten Markets
High Consumer Expectations
Cost Pressures

Hybrid Flexible Governance Models

Fig 5.1 Moving towards Flexible Governance Model

5.2 What is Blockchain Consortium Governance?

Blockchain governance refers to the mechanisms by which decentralized node networks adapt and change over time. This includes decisions like changes in block sizes, data storage formats, smart-contract execution protocol, consensus mechanism and more. In the context of a Blockchain Consortium, we define governance as a set of rules that govern this partnership, both organizational and operational. These rules focus on what is the subject of the regulation, who is involved, i.e. what their roles are, what they are responsible for and how decisions will be made. These rules can be code (e.g. Smart Contracts), laws (e.g. fees for malign actors), processes (what must be done when X happens), or responsibilities (who must do what).

5.3 Why is Good Governance Necessary for a Blockchain Consortium?

As the size and complexity of Blockchain Consortiums grows, the need for proper governance becomes critical for the long-term success of the Blockchain ecosystem. Since the strategic value of a Blockchain network lies in its scaling, it is important to consider that an increasing network size correlates positively with an increase in coordination complexity. Hence, a proper establishment of sustainable governance principles for the deployment of a Blockchain Consortium is key. As per Deloitte's latest 2020 global Blockchain survey, many consortiums that began with good intentions to help its members to succeed in their Blockchain-related endeavours often failed because of internal disputes and perceived inequities over issues related to the amount of funding and effort that the individual members commit, the amount of profit that members receive, etc. Due to this, many enterprises placed a solid emphasis on performing their due diligence and addressing key concerns related to governance concerns before agreeing to participate in the consortium. There are various reasons why good governance is necessary for a Blockchain Consortium – for successful scaling up and crossing of the chasms, as discussed below:

a) No single participant exerting dominant control:

Blockchain Consortiums have many of the same benefits of private Blockchains. But there is one prominent difference – they should employ a group governance model over their network, so no one party can exert dominant control over the others. This increases the trust of a consortium network significantly over a single entity, private Blockchain, while still maintaining the benefits of a private Blockchain. Additionally, consortium Blockchains are not restricted to only being visible to network members. Their transactions can be openly seen by the public, engendering increased trust.

b) Simplified governance can resolve the mystery of Coopetition Paradox:

For any organization, Blockchain adoption should not be a goal in itself but a means to achieve specific business benefits. The true power of Blockchain technology lies in its ability to enable peer-to-peer interactions and cross-enterprise automation – supported by Smart Contracts – typically as part of a broader solution. It offers an opportunity for greater trust and increased efficiency in value chains between the participants of the consortiums. These Blockchain Consortiums are thereby effectively obliged to address the so-called Coopetition Paradox through collaboration between natural competitors in a particular industry. The Coopetition Paradox forces Blockchain Consortiums to break up fierce competition between industry rivals in order to access the strategic value of such a business network. Obviously, there is no one-size-fits-all solution to this topic.

c) Robust governance diminishes dependence on incumbents:

In many ways, we end up depending on these incumbents globally for most of our online transactions and value transfer. Can we say we have become the prisoners of these centralized organizations? One of the important motivations to use Blockchain governance in a Blockchain Consortium is that it could mitigate indirect dependence on incumbents, such as Facebook, Amazon, Google, Microsoft that determine their own rules, like the publicly criticized use of personal data. Publicly accessible and governable Blockchains could mitigate that indirect dependence. Everybody who is interested in how those systems are set-up, could purchase the respective tokens and suggest changes including changes with regards to how personal data is handled.

5.4 Components of a Blockchain Consortium Governance

Well-designed, inclusive, and fair governance of a consortium is a core requirement to operate and maintain a distributed ledger solution. In the enterprise space, we must define a simplified governance framework, in which we create a governance model that is inclusive of the principles of collective behaviour theory, incentives, penalties, flexibility, delegation, and network mechanisms of coordination. A governance structure in a Blockchain network can include multiple levels of workgroups that should have a dedicated focus to address the following specific concerns:

1. The disruptive nature of the envisioned business model and its impact on participants

2. The roles and accountability of participants

3. Decision rights

4. Shared incentives and disincentives

5. IP rights and liabilities

6. Existing regulatory and compliance policies and awareness of future changes

7. Technical design and architecture

Governance for a Blockchain Consortium can typically be thought of in three separate components:

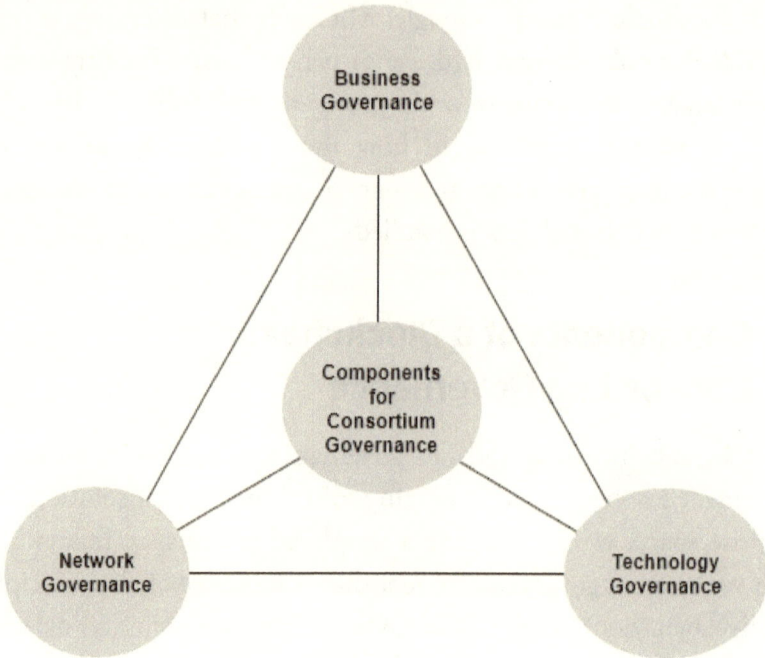

Fig 5.2 – Components of Blockchain Consortium Governance.

1. **Business governance**: This is a discipline that drives the industry and use case specific, multi-organizational operational structure, including forming a legal entity, establishing the governance model for the new legal entity, setting a budget, creating commercial models, allocating profits, costs, incentives, compliance and setting appropriate marketing strategy. One key goal of business

governance is to manage the growth of the consortium while maintaining the SLA and core business objectives. As Blockchain Consortiums evolve and grow, and as new participants are added or removed, the dynamics of the network change, and both bilateral and multilateral relationships may emerge.

2. **Technology governance**: This is a discipline that focuses on IT infrastructure, performance, cost structures, technology, and business risks. It includes a set of collaborative tools, processes, and methodologies intended to ensure organizational alignment of the business strategy with the technology infrastructure and services. This also includes setting information security and other standards for accessing the Blockchain solution, determining when participants must upgrade to a new version of the Blockchain software, and dispute resolution.

3. **Network Governance**: This involves ensuring effective network operations, including onboarding and off-boarding of participants, giving permissions to new network participants when they meet applicable standards, support services, risks and equitable cost structures distributed fairly, based on a consortium member's activities.

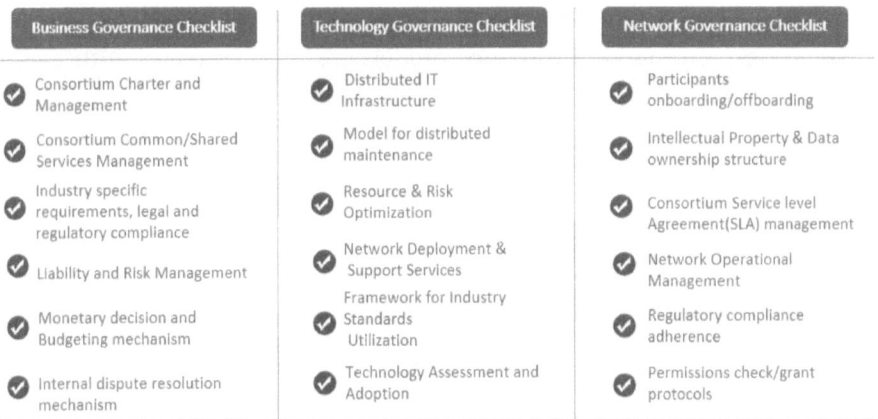

Business Governance Checklist	Technology Governance Checklist	Network Governance Checklist
Consortium Charter and Management	Distributed IT Infrastructure	Participants onboarding/offboarding
Consortium Common/Shared Services Management	Model for distributed maintenance	Intellectual Property & Data ownership structure
Industry specific requirements, legal and regulatory compliance	Resource & Risk Optimization	Consortium Service level Agreement(SLA) management
Liability and Risk Management	Network Deployment & Support Services	Network Operational Management
Monetary decision and Budgeting mechanism	Framework for Industry Standards Utilization	Regulatory compliance adherence
Internal dispute resolution mechanism	Technology Assessment and Adoption	Permissions check/grant protocols

Fig 5.3 Checklist for different components of Blockchain governance

5.5 Scaling Up the Blockchain Consortiums Through Robust Governance

"Governance is an essential component to any successful blockchain effort. The architecture, business process and data definition are all key to ensuring the right business value is delivered to key stakeholders"

Lee Slezak, Vice President – IT Architecture, Tyson Foods

Most of the decisions regarding innovation are generally carried out within the boundaries of a firm. But this same approach for innovation might not be fruitful or perhaps may even be futile here, as firms have little experience of sharing control or dealing with open source innovation. Shared Blockchain applications require coordination across firm boundaries. This requires a radically different approach to software governance because no single entity or individual can unilaterally make decisions regarding rule changes, code base upgrades, or record altering.

Enterprise Blockchains currently use a variety of governance models, with benefits for both, centralized and decentralized decision making – such as benevolent dictatorships, oligarchies, stakeocracies, federations, representative meritocracies, meritocracies, and democracies. Many of these above-mentioned governance models are supplemented with either steering or advisory committees that provide guidance, but don't have any formal decision making rights, but are, nonetheless, influential in guiding, recommending, and providing expertise on the development of the Blockchain. Often used in conjunction with centralized governance structures, steering/advisory committees help ensure that decisions are transparent (at least to the members). For instance, the IBM Food Trust, MediLedger, and TradeLens rely on such committees for direction.

Different stakeholders prefer different governance models and each governance model has its own advantages and disadvantages. Hence the development of the governance model is a challenging and emerging discipline in the enterprise Blockchain world. The governance structure and landscape determine the interaction models, growth (centralized or decentralized), technology design, and overall business operation of Blockchain Consortium network. There is a close-knit dependency between business models and governance structures that govern various facets of Blockchain Consortium operations. A well-crafted governance model will ensure balance and smooth interactions between various entities that compete with some network participants and that cooperate and co-create with some other network participants. Having said that, we must consider how different governance choices influence and incentivize each stakeholder's behaviour in the Blockchain Consortium network.

While the inherent nature of the Blockchain technology itself demands collaboration requiring competitors to collaborate to establish a viable ecosystem to support and drive future success, Blockchain Consortium governance needs a multidimensional approach factoring in aspects such as decision rights for defining various aspects of a Blockchain system, such as network access; data use; data ownership and control; the role of validator nodes; software updates; ledger overrides; funding models and more in a much more inclusive and holistic way. There is no one-size-fits-all model for Blockchain Consortium governance and hence it is imperative that Blockchain governance continues to evolve, often progressing from centralized to decentralized, and from simple to complex governance arrangements.

5.6 Blockchain Consortium Governance Models

Systemic governance that relies solely on incentives and network coordination is inadequate to address more highly structured and regulated industries and their use cases, especially in a Blockchain Consortium environment. The aim of the Blockchain Consortium governance is to define a simplified and evolving governance framework that draws inspiration from the core tenets of Blockchain design and incorporates a governance model that encompasses principles of game theory, incentives, penalties, flexibility, delegation, and network mechanisms of coordination.

For most of the successful Blockchain Consortiums operating today, governance is a work in progress and has varying degrees of decentralization. This degree of decentralization generally evolves based on mutually agreed dynamic business objectives and the number of participants existing in the consortium. When a Blockchain Consortium is formed by either an individual or by a small group, it generally adopts a centralized decision making governance style at an initial stage for the purpose of making swift decisions, quick execution, higher efficiency, clear control and accountability. But, because of the fact that centralized governance is antithetical to the principles and purposes of Blockchains which aim to dissipate power across the participants of the consortium, the founders then swiftly move towards having more decentralized governance in order to attract a critical mass of additional adopters.

Based on the formation of Blockchain applications and projects, the following governance structures operate in practice: benevolent dictatorships; oligarchies; stakeocracies; federations representative meritocracies; meritocracies; and democracies. (Refer to the table below)

Governance Model Name	Ownership of Voting / Decision Rights	Examples of Consortium
Benevolent Dictator	A single entity holds decision making rights even seeking inputs from others.	TRADELENS 1. Initially, Vitalik Buterin over the idea of Ethereum 2. Initially, Maersk over the Trade Finance Consortium "TradeLens"
Oligarchy	A few group of entities hold decision making rights while seeking inputs from all the other members in the consortium.	Satoshi Nakamoto willingly gave Martti Malmi and Gavin Andresen access rights to update Bitcoin's website and source code
Stakeocracy	In this type of governance model, organizations or people must pay to become a part of the oligarchy.	libra Libra Association refers to its decision-making process as "proportional power", where voting powers of the council will be proportional to their stake.
Federation	Decentralized groups specialize on parts of the project while coordinating with a central group	HYPERLEDGER The Hyperledger Project's overarching structure is a set of specialized projects
Representative Meritocracy	In this type of governance model, the stakeholders have to prove their merit to be eligible for election to the committee based on votes from other meritorious members.	HYPERLEDGER Technical Steering Committee is governed by 11 elected people from a pool of active contributors
Democracy	Any participant can vote	Bitcoin miners 'vote' by either installing or failing to install changes to the source code

Fig 5.4 – Different Governance Models with examples

a. **Benevolent Dictator Governance Model**: In this type of governance structure, control is often centralized to either the founder (if launched by an individual) or to a small group (if launched by a team). Classic examples of benevolent dictators are Satoshi Nakamoto himself, over the launch of Bitcoin Whitepaper and Bitcoin Core, and Vitalik Buterin over the idea for Ethereum. These projects succeeded because the earliest of adopters – typically other like-minded coders – trusted the founders' intentions, even in the interesting case of Bitcoin where the identity of Nakamoto was not known.

b. **Oligarchy Governance Model**: In this type of governance, control is usually in the hands of the few. Most Blockchain Consortiums are being developed by a core group of partners, sometimes referred to as the minimal viable ecosystem (MVE). These partners – often comprising competitors as well as trading partners – form some sort of a council charged with developing and enforcing the rules for the initiative. By their very nature, the rules represent a negotiated treaty among the founding partners, maximizing their benefits. Founders will likely need to alter rules of engagement as they seek to attract new partners in order to attract a critical mass of additional adopters.

c. **Stakeocracy Governance Model:** In this type of governance model, organizations or people have to pay to become a part of the oligarchy. A good example for this is LIBRA, the new digital currency project initiated by Facebook which is governed by the LIBRA Association. The council members of the LIBRA Association which comprises 28 members as of now, have to buy at least USD $10 million of LIBRA investment tokens. LIBRA Association refers to its decision making process as 'proportional power', where the voting powers of the council will be proportional to their stake, but with a cap to prevent an overtaking of the LIBRA Association.

d. **Federation Governance Model:** This type of governance structure allows decentralized groups to specialize on parts of the project while coordinating with a central organizing group to integrate solutions. An example for this is Hyperledger Project's overarching structure where a set of specialized projects are coordinated by a centralized steering committee.

e. **Representative Meritocracy Governance Model:** In this type of governance model, the stakeholders have to prove their merit to be eligible for election to the committee, based on votes from other meritorious members. A good example of this is Hyperledger's Technical Steering Committee which follows the ABCs of open governance. Working group leaders for Hyperledger's projects submit active contributors (there were 424 as of the last election) and all active participants vote to elect the 11 leaders. The 11-person Technical Steering Committee (TSC) has decision making rights over the admission of new projects, rules over projects, and status of projects (incubation/active).

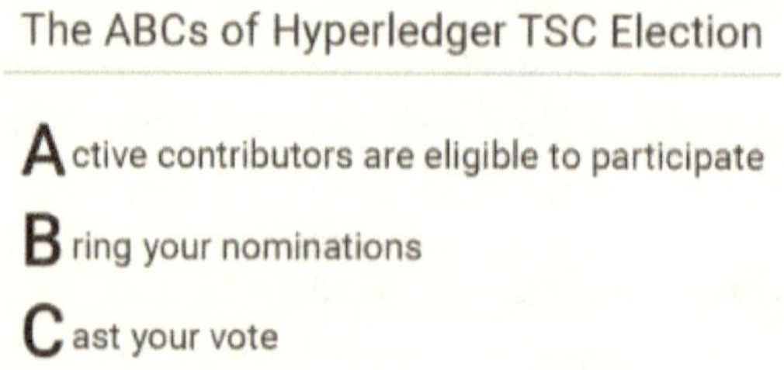

The ABCs of Hyperledger TSC Election

A ctive contributors are eligible to participate

B ring your nominations

C ast your vote

Fig 5.5 – Hyperledger ABC Open Governance model

f. **Meritocracy Governance Model:** In this type of governance model where the power is held by many people based on one's ability (and goodwill), seems the ideal many strive for, particularly in open source projects. The aim is to elicit multiple views from informed stakeholders, debate views in open forums, and then stress-test ideas to find the best solution.

g. **Democracy Governance Model:** This type of governance model is the most decentralized form of governance, where every consortium participant gets to vote. A good example of this is Bitcoin's Elegant Upgrade Mechanism. If a majority of Bitcoin miners 'vote' for a particular upgrade, then, by definition, this is the new version of Bitcoin. That's why many people like the fact that Bitcoin miners 'vote' by either installing or failing to install changes to the source code.

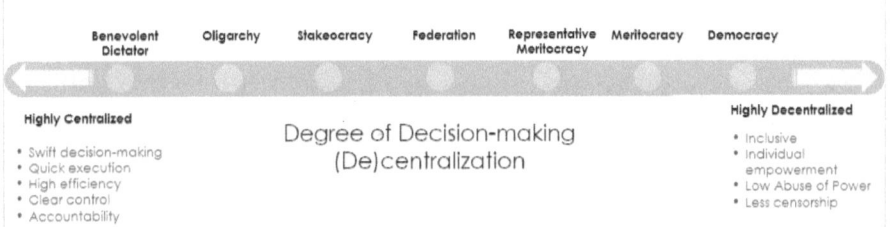

Fig 5.6 – Blockchain Governance Models

In summary, there are a number of Blockchain governance models. For a given Blockchain ecosystem, several structures may be used because governance over a Blockchain ecosystem is complex and ever-evolving.

5.7 Facets of Blockchain Consortium Governance

Consortiums need clear governance rules. Each facet may be overseen by a different governance model, forming a governance portfolio. A comprehensive governance portfolio needs to provide answers to the following important questions, such as:

- Do all network members have equal voting rights, or is there a tiered membership?

- Do voting network members pay for their position in the voting pool, or do leaders get elected to voting positions?

- Are the rules based on a majority, a plurality, or unanimity?

- Who decides what patches and functionality will be added and when? How are software changes distributed to nodes?

- Who is allowed to submit counter transactions which essentially reverse transactions? Who is authorized to roll back the ledger in the instance of egregious errors? (i.e. Who has the power to create a hard fork?)

- How is the board structured?

- How are objections or concerns arbitrated?

- Do the rules apply across the entire consortium, or do some rules apply only to some teams or initiatives, as is the case with the Hyperledger project?

- How are the rules updated as business and technology contexts change? Who funds the project?

- Who decides who pays what? Who decides the pricing model (including transaction fees)?

Regardless of the answers to these questions, a consortium could use a Blockchain solution in various ways to operate the organization, document the rules, and enforce them. Blockchain governance is multifaceted. A governance portfolio should address questions related to the below given facets:

Key Facets of Blockchain Consortium Governance

Fig 5.7 – Facets of Blockchain Governance

a) Purpose

> TradeLens has different types of participants, such as network members, cargo owners, clients, financial institutions. Our approach was to try and make sure that we had a unique value proposition and rules crafted for each different category of network member.
>
> Aaron Lieber, Head of Offering Management, TradeLens, IBM.

A formal purpose statement should express the aspirations and values of the Blockchain Consortium. A compelling mission can keep members engaged, particularly when facing significant obstacles and can inspire others to join the network. In general, a mission should appeal to a greater good beyond the founders. For e.g., the mission statement of TradeLens – a Blockchain Consortiums for the shipping industry reads: "*TradeLens is an open and neutral platform to help set trade free. TradeLens is a platform for digitizing and transforming trade for the benefit of industry and authorities all along the global supply chain. It offers a more open, trusted, transparent and secure way to conduct the business of trade.*"

b) Rights of Membership

For efficient functioning of a Blockchain Consortium, the members must decide how they will be represented in the consortium and how the governing board will be structured. The major issues to decide on in relation to consortium governance are: size, method of appointment or elections, term of mandate, quorum (the number of board members needed to transact business), percentage votes for approval (and any special percentages for certain decisions), appointment of officers and affiliated entity board limits. The participants of the Blockchain Consortium are generally categorized as "Consortium Members" – members of the corporate entity or parties to the contractual arrangement that are involved in its business governance – and "network participants" – refers to users of the Blockchain network that are involved in operational governance. For example, consortium members will be interested in business aspects of governance such as budget and financials, ownership of IP, and management of the network as a whole. Network participants will be interested in dispute resolution, requirements for participation, and information security standards.

Rights of Membership which includes a gamut of rights such as participation, validation, override and liability are necessary to consider how a Blockchain Consortium's members decide on voting power in the consortium for technical/political decisions, strategy and roadmap. Rights of participation for network participants define who will be allowed to submit transactions to the Blockchain Consortium network. At a very high level, rights of participation are either open to the public or private. Rights of validation define who is allowed to run validator nodes in the Blockchain Consortium network. Given the immutable nature of Blockchains, consideration should also be given as to whether there are any circumstances in which network participants will be required to reverse a transaction or refrain from completing a partial transaction. In that case, the right to override should be appropriately assigned to members in the consortium who are allowed to submit counter transactions – which essentially reverse transactions – and who are authorized to roll back the ledger in in cases of egregious errors, i.e. who has the power to create a hard fork.

The rights of participation and validation may vary by stakeholder type and depend on the type of Blockchain network chosen as shown here:

		Network Participants who can view, decipher data or submit Transactions	
		Permissioned (This requires rights for permission, selection or election)	Permissionless (Open to Public and Anyone can do transaction)
Network Participants who can operate a validator node	Private (requires Key to access)	Private - Permissioned MediLedger IBM Food Trust TRADELENS	Private - Permissionless (Hybrid Blockchain Solution) EY Ops Chain Public Edition (under development)
	Public (Anyone)	Public - Permissioned ripple libra EOS	Public - Permissionless bitcoin ethereum Monero

Fig 5.8 – Right of Participation matrix – Private/Public Blockchain

c) Data Governance

The perceived loss of control over data is one of the biggest obstacles to Blockchain adoption that many organizations face. With good project planning and communication however, this issue can be greatly mitigated. A well-designed data governance model should clearly specify data policies, such as:

- What data is collected?

- Who can view the data?

- Who decides how data can be used?

- Type of data storage mechanism

Governance should define who owns the data on a shared ledger; who owns the software; and who is liable if the law is broken or if a regulation is not followed. For example, the public address data on the Public Blockchain is public, and the private keys are meant to only be in the possession of the legitimate owner. For private Blockchains, most enterprise Blockchain applications seem to operate under this rule: the organization that uploaded the data, owns the data and controls access to it. The table below provides examples of data ownership policies and software ownership for MediLedger, IBM Food Trust, and TradeLens.

Consortium Name	Data Ownership Policy	Software Ownership
MediLedger	Data is owned by the Company - By leveraging the blockchain and confidential data exchange, the Network is designed to ensure that each Participant's Private Data is owned by such Participant, and each Participant has full control of who and how it shares its Private Data.	Chronicled owns the platform
IBM Food Trust™	Data is owned by the registered company or organization that owns the data prior to it being uploaded to Food Trust.	IBM owns the Food Trust Platform
TRADELENS	A channel will be established for each node hosting organization. Sensitive information including documents are distributed only to those nodes participating in a channel.	Maersk owns the intellectual property of the TradeLens platform

Fig 5.9 – Data and Software Ownership Examples in Blockchain Consortium

To increase data privacy, some permissionless Blockchains like Monero and Zcash use advanced cryptography techniques like ring signatures, zero knowledge proofs, and key images, which allow only the parties access to a particular transaction to decipher data and access to funds stored on the Blockchain, even when posted on a Public Blockchain.

d) Software Control

One of the main governance challenges for a shared application is software update control. In a collaborative environment, agreeing upon system upgrades and maintenance can become a complicated task among stakeholders. Maintenance and upgrades of Blockchain systems are vital to any successful effort. Decentralized software updates require a lot of planning and coordination. Participants in a Blockchain Consortium may have different processes for how upgrades and maintenance internally occur, leading to a lack of agreement among stakeholders as a whole. In order to prevent gridlock or delays in development of the technology, a strong technical committee with representation from relevant stakeholder groups should oversee the decisions as to when changes should be implemented. If the Blockchain Consortium is developing its own Blockchain protocol or applications, members will need to consider how code is managed. Who has control of the official codebase? Who has the right to request changes? Who decides what changes to make? How are changes propagated across the network? Versioning should be defined and maintained separately from any member organization's specific IT components. This will be important as upgrades are introduced across the network.

e) Sustainable Governance Framework

Consortiums need a sustainable governance framework that is contractually binding on all participants and clearly sets out each party's rights and responsibilities. The governance can be off-chain, on-chain, or a combination of both. Off-chain governance is alterable, allowing the governance model to evolve over time. Most Blockchain governance is managed off-chain, whether its decisions are over source code patches or updates, protocol changes, or membership changes. Off-chain governance is the lower-risk option. On-chain governance is unalterable without a significant software fork or intervention approved by the majority of the participants (e.g. EOS , DFINITY, Tezos).

f) Consortium Financing

Money is a constant challenge for consortiums, which have to balance the need for sustainable funding with expectations around access and control. So one of the most important considerations for organizations planning to participate in a Blockchain Consortium is to have crystal clear clarity on funding requirements. For a question, such as: "How much does it cost to join a Blockchain Consortium?" The obvious answer is, "It depends".

Based on the data collected from Ledger Insights about the specifics of four large initiatives (VAKT, Komgo, We.Trade and B3i), it was found that the current funding for those projects ranged from $6.3m to $33m, averaging $1.2 million per member. As companies remain tight-lipped about their investments in Blockchain initiatives including consortiums, anecdotal evidence indicates a price tag between $500,000 to $1 million for the first 1-2 years in start-up funding by member investors. So it's important for consortiums to clarify these factors in balancing financial flexibility with auditability for consortiums.

	Enterprise blockchain membership costs			
	Sector	Members	Funding	Average $ per member
VAKT	Energy post trade	12	$33m	$2.75m
komgo	Trade finance	15	$15m	$1m
we.trade	Trade finance	12	$8.1m	$680,000
B3i	Insurance	13	$6.3m	$480,000

Fig 5.10 – Typical Enterprises Membership Costs – Source Ledger Insights

5.8 Blockchain Consortiums Risk Factors

> No technology, including blockchain, is without risk. The long-term winners in the blockchain space know how to recognize the risk, quantify the risk, and manage the risk in a blockchain-based application.
>
> Michael Prokop, Blockchain Leader, Deloitte US Risk & Financial Advisory

New technologies carry potential downsides that need to be identified and managed. This is especially true when that technology is not merely an overlaying application but rather a core part of the organization's underlying IT infrastructure, as is often the case with Blockchain. Organizations should adopt a proactive approach in recognizing new risks stemming from Blockchain. Risk management should not be an afterthought; rather, it should be hardwired into the consideration set from the initial scoping and strategy phase of a Blockchain project itself. While this list of potential risks might seem rather long and daunting, many of these pitfalls are ones your organization is likely to face in the implementation of any other new technology as well. The key challenges are – choosing the right scope, having the right motivation for a business and its participants, ensuring the right governance structure, and having the correct team and technology in place. These challenges can be conquered if you make deliberate and diligent efforts to manage the Blockchain network effectively and focus on driving the ultimate transformation that you envisioned. The common risks stemming from a Blockchain Consortium network can be sorted into five broad categories:

a. **Technology Risks**

Effective development and deployment of a consortium's Blockchain-based solutions require the identification and addressing of a list of technological risks and challenges. Many businesses might be overwhelmed by the technical challenges regarding privacy, scale, or throughput, such as the number of transactions, interoperability, consensus, contract verification, tools, support, integration-related issues with other enterprise systems and quantum computing threats.

b. **Strategic Risks**

Adoption of Blockchain technologies and consortium business models is a strategic bet for organizations. It thus entails a range of strategic questions, such as defining the applicable Value Proposition, brand and reputation management, and handling change management.

c. **Operational Risks**

Certain risks are inherent to the nature of Blockchain technology. Implementation of Blockchain-based applications, especially in a consortium of several organizations, is complex and involves addressing a number of operational risk issues such as governance, controls, auditability of Blockchain transactions, and proof-of-assets ownership. As consortiums move forward with caution, it is recommended that business leaders evaluate each operational risk to determine if: (a) they have already turned into specific issues for them today – if so, determine mitigating actions that consortium needs to take; or (b) they will remain risks – if so, how they will monitor them throughout the project and address them should they manifest.

d. **Financial Risks**

A common aim of Blockchain Consortium deployment is to facilitate transfers of value. A variety of financial risks need to be considered while designing such Blockchain applications, platforms, and infrastructure, such as potential for financial loss, transaction settlement finality, consortium funding-related risks, and IP protection issues. In addition, there are a number of accounting and reporting challenges that should be considered when depending on Blockchain-based applications for financial transactions and for information used in financial reporting

e. **Legal and Regulatory Risks**

Blockchain as a technology may not be regulated, but applications built using Blockchain technology will need to adhere to relevant regulations, such as the European Union's General Data Protection Regulation (GDPR) relating to data protection and privacy. Legal and regulatory risks include uncertainty around cross-jurisdictional regulations, antitrust violations, smart-contract enforceability, anti-money laundering (AML) and KYC, and IP protection.

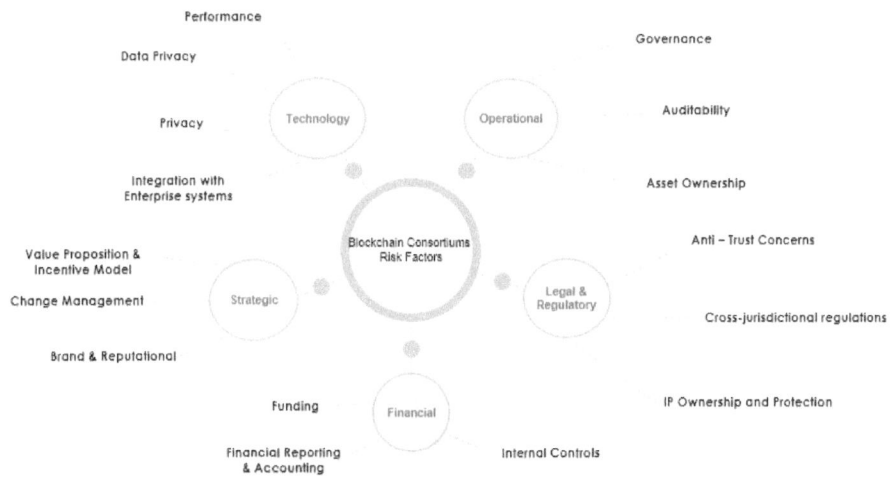

Fig 5.11 – Blockchain Consortium Risk Factors

A Global Blockchain Survey 2018 conducted by Deloitte, suggested that the vast majority of respondents (74 percent) said that they either already participate in or are likely to join a Blockchain Consortium. Many enterprises are highly interested in joining these consortiums in order to gain optimal benefits of this technology. Joining such a Blockchain Consortium could bring enterprises a number of interesting benefits, including cost savings, shared (and lower) risks, building critical mass of adoption, and offer influencing standards. As these consortiums are mainly suited for specific business purposes, enterprises can easily link these up with their existing network more efficiently than public or private Blockchain. This can lead to shorter development times and economies of scale. However, there is still a large uncertainty among them on how these consortiums work and how they are governed. Up until recently, the focus was mainly on governance solutions for Public Blockchain platforms like Hyperledger and Ethereum. Consortium Blockchain governance however will become as or even more important to enterprises than Public Blockchain governance because they will work with this level of governance on a daily basis.

Q: Which of the following best describes your organization's position on participating in a blockchain consortium with competitors?

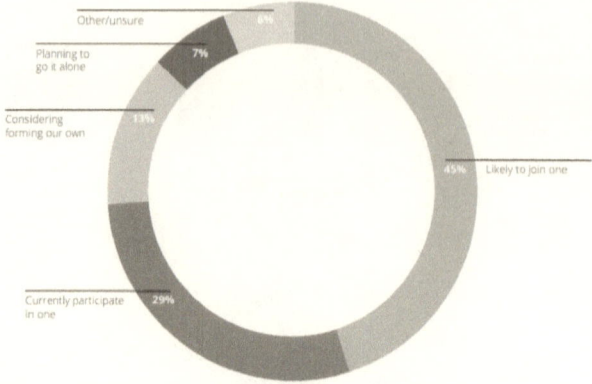

Fig 5.12 – Deloitte Global Blockchain Survey 2018

Yet, the difficulties in working with other firms in an ecosystem is one of the biggest barriers to Blockchain adoption (PwC, 2018). In another study, the World Economic Forum and the United Arab Emirates (Al Olama, 2020) report found that the top three challenges to Blockchain implementation for corporations and service providers are unclear regulatory implications, difficulty in bringing together the required stakeholders, and educating and enhancing awareness of the involved stakeholders. McKinsey cites similar concerns in their report that: "There must be a governance agreement covering participation, ownership, maintenance, compliance, and data standards". A paper on consortium governance by Radcliffe (2019) also discusses the differences between permissioned and public Blockchains, finding that cooperative governance agreements for permissioned Blockchains require daily attention to maintain high levels of trust and cooperative behaviour between the parties.

5.9 Blockchain Consortium's Challenges

Blockchain ecosystems are, by their very nature, a shared resource for firms, but how consortium partners collaborate to successfully adopt Blockchain is an emerging study. These can be complicated relationships to navigate because of overlapping roles; one can simultaneously be a competitor, a supplier, or a customer. The ability to understand how to respect boundaries in a shared environment is difficult for firms used to guarding their resources protectively. It's important for consortium participants to begin the conversation with a consensus definition of collaborative governance. Before focusing on the long-term vision of distributed governance, the consortium has to ensure that it can run successfully in the short term. A stable governance mechanism has to be in place to keep the consortium functioning and to evaluate if the necessary collaboration was achievable on a small scale and could still be achieved when more members join in, in the future. A recent 2020 Global Blockchain Survey from Deloitte suggests that consortiums face a full array of challenges in attracting new members, with rules and participants, roles and responsibilities heralding the list. This trend is expected to continue for the foreseeable future, as increased acceptance of the consortium model is crucial to the overall success and growth of Blockchain-enabled solutions across business sectors.

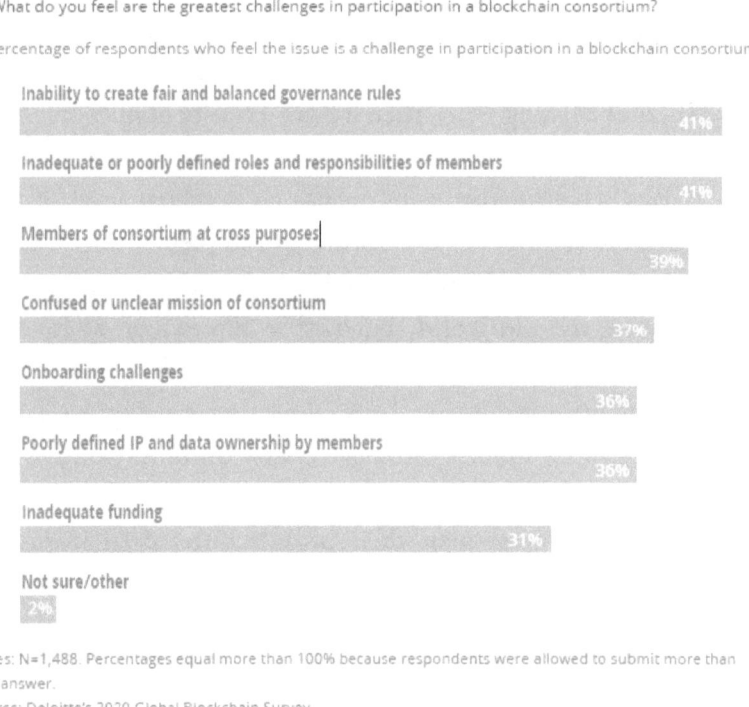

Q. What do you feel are the greatest challenges in participation in a blockchain consortium?

Percentage of respondents who feel the issue is a challenge in participation in a blockchain consortium

Inability to create fair and balanced governance rules
41%

Inadequate or poorly defined roles and responsibilities of members
41%

Members of consortium at cross purposes
39%

Confused or unclear mission of consortium
37%

Onboarding challenges
36%

Poorly defined IP and data ownership by members
36%

Inadequate funding
31%

Not sure/other
2%

Notes: N=1,488. Percentages equal more than 100% because respondents were allowed to submit more than one answer.
Source: Deloitte's 2020 Global Blockchain Survey.

Fig 5.13 – Survey Question result from Deloitte 2020 Global Blockchain Survey

To make the most of the benefits and the evolving business relationships from the consortiums, business leaders need to have crystal clarity on the following important topics while deciding to join a Blockchain Consortium.

a. Clarity of Purpose – *Why are you here?*

Every enterprise should be clear about their goals when contemplating joining a Blockchain Consortium. Joining to study and explore Blockchain technology is a very different commitment from aggressively moving to build and deploy the technology on a commercial scale. Hence industry players should have dual-purpose clarity: Firstly clarity on the business rationale and objectives of the enterprise itself – a specific business problem to start with before deciding to join a Blockchain Consortium. And secondly, understanding the goals of the consortium itself and evaluating them to see if they align with the business goals of the individual organization as well. Most organizations lack this clarity and end up with failed initiatives or missed expectations. If the Blockchain Consortium itself is conceived because of FOMO (Fear of Missing Out), then it has no clarity of purpose (its level of risk on this issue is therefore greatest). Whereas a consortium with a Blockchain-native solution has an excellent level of clarity of governance (low risk). Creating and implementing a Blockchain solution is not a traditional IT build. There's no point in re-creating the old world, but with a Blockchain at its core. The danger in not recognizing this paradigm shift from the outset, is that organizations end up reasserting existing roles, processes and business models. Strategic clarity on both fronts will ensure that the Blockchain initiative has a business purpose and business leaders can then plan their organization's participation in the Blockchain Consortium to reap its true benefits.

b. Clarity of Funding – *Who pays for what in the consortium?*

Consortiums will play a central role in the commercialization of Blockchain technology in every industry. We can expect dozens more consortiums to form in the next two or three years. Not all will lead to commercial deployments, and this is fine for members who are more interested in learning at this stage. Companies with serious commercial intent will want to consider the funding, membership, leadership, and governance of the consortiums they join. Money is a constant challenge for consortiums, which have to balance the need for sustainable funding with expectations around access and control. So one of the most important considerations for organizations planning to participate in a Blockchain Consortium is to have crystal clear clarity on funding requirements.

c. Clarity of IP & Data Ownership – *Who owns what in the consortium ?*

To truly unlock the potential of Blockchain, the underlying technology, including its software, will have to be shared in order for value to be gained. The nature of such 'sharing' depends entirely on the specific nature of the Blockchain Consortium in question, including its purposes, subject matter, and relationship between the Blockchain participants. It is therefore important to consider questions around the nature of the underlying IP, IP and data ownership and licensing arrangement as part of the structuring of the Blockchain. To create an environment of participation and openness, business leaders need to have clarity on which intellectual assets belong to participant organizations and which belong to the consortium, along with clearly defined rules for data ownership and stewardship. For this reason, IP creation, donation, and data monetization should be well defined.

d. Clarity of Technology Sourcing – *How will technology decisions be made?*

Blockchain Consortiums often conduct pilot projects, and many of these efforts involve third-party technology vendors or service providers. The need for outside expertise raises important questions about how technology will be selected and paid for, and how to avoid vendor bias by powerful members. When a consortium-built technology platform does not fit into the broader architecture of individual members, the members incur additional costs and operational issues. So it's imperative for the business leaders to know precisely how the Blockchain Consortium will handle big technology-related decisions and also, how the consortium will factor in the kind of implications that the technology selection may have on an individual enterprise's security policy.

e. Clarity on Governance – *How will decision making happen in the consortium?*

Blockchain governance refers to the mechanisms by which decentralized node networks adapt and change over time. This includes decisions like changes in block sizes, data storage formats, smart-contract execution protocol, consensus mechanism, and more. Blockchain governance is a novel and complex issue, and there is still no consensus regarding the best ways to address it. Deciding on a governance model is important at the very formation of a consortium, as the governance model is key for all other decision making. So having clarity on the overall governance framework including on-chain and off-chain protocols is an essential activity for the business leaders to embark upon, before deciding whether to join the consortium or not.

f. Clarity on Exit Strategy – *How does one exit from the consortium?*

Blockchain Consortium have generally well-defined rules on how members can participate, but rarely do they have a clear cut exit plan for members, when a consortium's goals no longer align with a member's goals. It is necessary for business leaders to understand both the entry and the exit rules so that they can decide whether the risks of potential lock-in are worth the gains of participation. A well-crafted exit strategy for the Blockchain Consortium allows the member participants to define the boundaries of their financial, technological, process, and data commitment to the consortium, and finally, what to do when the goals of the consortiums no longer fit with a member organization's priorities.

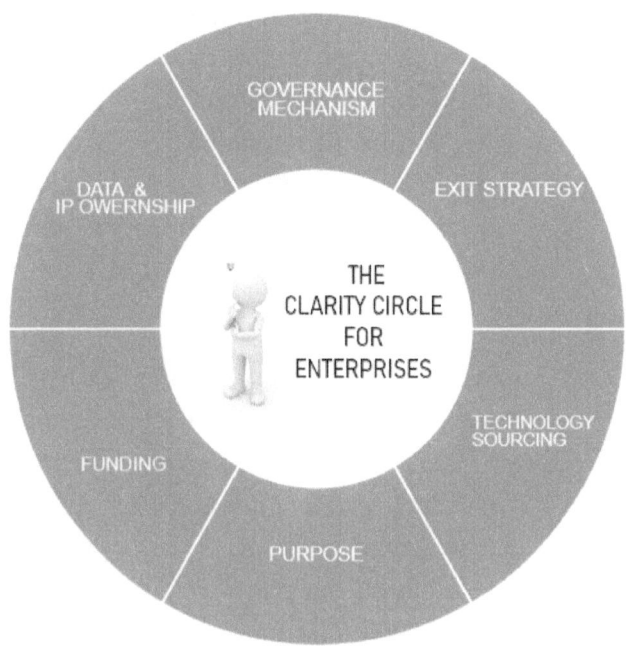

Fig 5.14 – The Clarity Circle for Enterprises – Key Considerations

5.10 Blockchain Consortiums Collaborative Governance Model – Suggestive Framework

> Ecosystems require managers to think about business challenges in a new way. The traditional focus on maximizing profits within the boundaries of the company may be the very thing that keeps companies from engaging and succeeding with participation in an ecosystem.
>
> Jesper Mathias Nielsen, Manager, Deloitte

Blockchain Consortiums are at an embryonic stage. They provide access to larger networks and relationships that offer a potential opportunity to do more with Blockchain than is possible within most individual organizations, but only for those with a high tolerance for ambiguity and uncertain reward. For a sound Blockchain Consortium, the permanence of the platform, impeccable credentials, fair and impartially foolproof governance with utmost trust is the most important attribute. A Blockchain ecosystem isn't likely to get off the ground without strong management support, and indeed, the most important role of collaborative leadership to bring disparate groups of stakeholders together and get them to buy-in to a common agenda. Other important considerations include the need for mutually agreed success metrics and a team of experts composed of members from all partners, that report to an "ecosystem board." This specialist team can not only ensure a sense of fair play for all firms but can also reinforce the unique nature of the ecosystem, itself a potential form of competitive advantage.

There are many forms and structures for building a bespoke ecosystem governance management model. Choosing a deliberate and business-driven approach will not only reduce the complexity and confusion of governance decisions, but will also reduce rework and maximize time-to-value of the ecosystem. The role of collaborative governance in shared value generation or a response to the "what's in it for me" is also considered important, and should be part of a Blockchain governance model: Most of the SMEs generally find it difficult to navigate the challenges in Blockchain governance, and hence there is a greater need for a large "anchor tenant" to set the direction for the rest of the ecosystem partners. An overarching Blockchain governance model assists in the consortium design and decision making. Hence, how to effectively collaborate amongst consortium partners emerged as a key inhibitor to Blockchain adoption. This cross-firm collaboration centred around governance concerns, and a lack of governance models as a missing but necessary link for Blockchain deployment. These models are crucial to firms who must intensely collaborate in a way that Blockchain requires. The meshed ecosystem that is Blockchain, means working in a many-to-many relationship (as opposed to a binary one), in novel ways. Thus, the lack of proper governance frameworks to assist necessary collaborative behaviour becomes the core of many failed Blockchain deployment projects. Below is a three-tier suggested framework to conceptualize an evolving governing framework for a Blockchain Consortium.

a. **Strategy Tier**

Here, enterprises set the strategic direction for Blockchain which includes business alignment, digital ambitions and future goals and also determines appropriate business scenarios, ideal use cases and the participants in the ecosystem.

b. **Business Model Tier**

Here the focus is mainly on the consortium structure and the type of the business model deployed. The most commonly used consortium business models today are broadly classified as Non-profit, For-Profit and the Traditional Utility business model. A right selection of the business model in this tier, based on the unique considerations of the consortium members, helps create sufficient value for the participants.

c. **Governance Model Tier**

The governance model tier should generally address the following concerns: ensure that all stakeholder groups in the Blockchain ecosystem are represented, focus on implementation of the business model for the consortium (business to business, business to consumer), determine IP ownership and licensing, and determine how to raise and spend funds to support the Blockchain project. Based on the type of Blockchain Consortiums, the following governance structures operate in practice: benevolent dictatorships, oligarchies, stakeocracies, federations representative meritocracies, meritocracies and democracies.

5.11 Rapid Checklist for Effective Consortium Governance Establishment

The quick checklist below may be useful as a good conversation starter within the consortium, regarding the establishment of a governance structure and governance issues around the day-to-day operation of a consortium. However, this list is not exhaustive; additional considerations are likely to come up in discussions of your particular use case, dispute resolution, data handling, and other issues that may arise anytime a new technology begins scaling up its user base. This list focuses on the most common business and operational governance considerations that have arisen in industry consortiums till date.

- **Organizational Structure of the Consortium:**

  - What are the key roles and responsibilities defined in the consortium charter and who will fill those positions?

  - How will the voting happen from each consortium member for any major decision related to the consortium?

  - How will the consortium engage with regulators?

  - How many members will be needed in the Blockchain Consortium?

- **Liability and Risk Management Mechanisms:**

  - What kind of insurance levels will be appropriate at the consortium entity level and whether the individual member insurance policies cover consortium-related work.

- **Consortium's Financial Strategy Considerations:**

  - How is the consortium initially funded and what commitments will consortium members have to make related to funding in the future, if additional funding is needed?

  - What is the ideal business revenue model for the consortium – Founder-led, Partnership-driven, Industry-driven, For-profit, not-for-profit or market utility?

  - What is the consortium's fee structure? Is it a licence, a subscription, a usage-based fee, or something else?

- **Consortium's Mission and the Value-creation Mechanism:**

  - What value will we deliver to consortium members and network participants?

  - What kind of mechanisms are needed to align incentives of various stakeholder groups?

  - How do you define KPI metrics for determining success in the short term and in the long term ?

  - What kind of mechanisms will be considered to audit the skills of consortium members at regular intervals to identify strengths and undertake gap analysis for continuous improvement of a consortium's services?

- **Participants On-boarding and Off-boarding:**

  - How will new participants join the consortium and what mechanisms are in place for approving new participants?

  - How will a participant's exit from the consortium be handled? How will the assets and transactions of the participant's transition upon exit?

- **Dispute Resolution and Error Handling Mechanisms:**

  - How will be a dispute be handled if there are disagreements among the consortium's participants?

  - What kind of transaction rollback/cancellation/error policy is in place to deal with faulty transactions?

- **Consortium Change Management:**

  - How will decisions regarding software upgrades at the strategic and operational level be made?

  - What kind of change management methodology will be deployed for system changes?

- **Data Management and IP Ownership Mechanisms:**

  - How will the data be stored and transmitted using the Blockchain solution?

  - What kind of data goes on-chain versus off-chain ?

  - What kind of data storage will be deployed? Centralized, decentralized or stored by the data owner with retrieval on-demand?

  - Are there appropriate protocols in place for data confidentiality and privacy?

  - Is there an agreement among the participants on how to document and handle the ownership of IP assets created in collaboration?

Making Business Sense of Blockchain Consortium

6.1 Overview – Business Model for Consortiums

Platform thinking has redefined business and given us some of today's most valuable companies. Everyone knows Amazon, Uber, Twitter and Alibaba, but not everyone understands the platform business model that powers their success. With the global emergence of Blockchain Consortiums, it is quite natural for collaborating firms to gravitate towards Platform business models. According to Deloitte, a Platform business model is one that focuses on helping to facilitate interactions across many participants in the vertical or horizontal ecosystem. Platform models in Blockchain have the ability to create value by connecting participants and creating fundamentally new markets, discovering value that was not previously available. From an investor's perspective, it's important to have a clear understanding of the proposed Blockchain Consortium before deciding to invest millions.

Blockchain technologies offer many possibilities to grow entirely new businesses and pose direct threats of disruption to traditional incumbents. Organizations using conventional business models built on the prediction of acting as an intermediary between two transaction parties must ask themselves if and how Blockchain technologies may impact their Value Propositions, how they compete, and how they operate.

In this chapter, we will synthesize our learning so far into a very specific tool called a Consortium Opportunity Analysis using a business model canvas. This tool will help anyone who wants to conceptualize and imagine key processes while starting a consortium. The goals of Consortium Opportunity Analysis are twofold: One, it's for you to identify a specific need or problem in your chosen industry that can potentially be solved using Blockchain technology. Two, it's for you to investigate possible solutions to this problem, including how these solutions might be executed.

6.2 Consortium Opportunity Analysis – Business Model Canvas

Blockchain Business Model Canvas allows promoters of a consortium to break down their proposed business model into easily-understood segments: The nine building blocks adapted from the business model framework given by Osterwalder and Pignuer are key to building the components for the Consortium Opportunity Analysis canvas. Let us understand each of the blocks in detail first.

a. Key Partners: **Who will help you?**

The Key Partnerships Building Block describes the network of suppliers and partners that make the business model work. To make the Blockchain initiative a success, Enterprises must forge partnerships and these collaborations are becoming a cornerstone of Blockchain Consortium business models. These partnerships may take forms such as strategic alliances, joint ventures, or buyer supplier relationships to ensure reliable supplies. The use of Blockchain can also enable the addition of new partners such as technology companies that develop Application Programming Interfaces (APIs) and Software Development Kits (SDKs). Enterprises create alliances to optimize their business models, reduce risk, or acquire resources.

b. Key Activities – **What is to be done?**

The Key Activities Building Block describes the most important things a consortium must do to make its business model work.

These are the most important actions a consortium must take to operate successfully. From a consortium's viewpoint, the Key Activities in this category relate to: platform management, service provisioning, and platform promotion. For instance, the Trade lens consortium applied the platform model to the supply chain which means bringing together an ecosystem of participants to create a lot of data about shipments. The ecosystem benefited all participants by revealing the shipments from their source, visibility of trade documentation, integrating sensor reading data. This provided incredible insights and enabled participants up and down the supply chain to use the data for their specific needs.

c.   Key Resources – **What do you need?**

The Key Resources building block describes the most important assets required to make a business model work. These resources allow an enterprise to create and offer a Value Proposition, reach markets, maintain relationships with customer segments, and earn revenues. Different Key Resources are needed depending on the type of business model. For example, in the case of the global supply chain consortium, TradeLens, three key technology resources that make the TradeLens consortium platform possible today are as follows:

a.   Firstly, Blockchain protocol which provides the means for securely storing, structuring, sharing and collaborating on the digital document workflow.

b.   Secondly, Cloud computing which enables infinite scalability.

c.   And finally, APIs which enable fluency between differing systems and software.

d.   Value Propositions – **What core value do you deliver to your audience?**

The Value Propositions building block describes the bundle of products and services that create value for a specific customer segment. The Value Proposition is the reason why customers turn to one company over another. For a consortium, the key questions to which investors might want to know the answers would be –

a. What value does the consortium deliver to its members?

b. What industry problems is the consortium trying to solve?

c. What bundles of products and services is the consortium offering to each customer segment?

In this sense, the Value Proposition is an aggregation, or bundle, of benefits that a consortium offers to its participants network.. Some Value Propositions may be innovative and represent a new or disruptive offer. Others may be similar to existing market offers, but with added features and attributes such as enhanced performance, newness, customization, cost reduction, increased convenience etc.

e. Customer Relationships – **How do you interact?**

The Customer Relationship Building Block "describes the types of relationships that an organization establishes with specific customer segments". These relationships may be driven by a motivation to acquire customers, to retain customers, or to boost sales. Consortiums should clarify the type of relationship they wants to establish with each customer segment. Relationships can range from personal to automated. Key Questions to be asked while determining the customer relationships are:

a. What type of relationship does each customer segment expect the consortium to establish and maintain?

b. How are they integrated with the rest of our business model?

f. Channels – **How do you reach them?**

The Channels Building Block describes how a company communicates with and reaches its customer segments to deliver a Value Proposition. These channels may be the consortium's own sales force, website, or the channels of its partners or wholesalers. One impact of using Blockchain is the simplification of doing business. Middle parties may become disintermediated. It serves as an interface between the consortium and its customers and plays a critical role in the user experience.

The key questions which needs to be checked here are:

a. Through which channels do the customer segments want to be reached?

b. How are the channels integrated? Which ones work best?

c. Which ones are most cost-efficient?

g. Customer Segments – **Who do you help?**

The Customer Segments Building Block defines the different groups of people or organizations that the consortium aims to reach and serve. The Blockchain Consortium must make a conscious decision about which customer segments to serve and which segments to ignore. Once this decision is made, a business model can be carefully designed around a strong understanding of specific customer needs. It is important to lock-in the customer segment early on so that right participants can join the consortium for it to grow.

h. Cost Structure – **What will it cost?**

The Cost Structure describes all costs incurred to operate a Blockchain Consortium. This building block describes the most important costs incurred while operating under a particular business model. Creating and delivering value, maintaining customer/member relationships, and generating revenue all incur costs.

i. Revenue Streams – **What are your earnings?**

The final and most important block is the Revenue Streams Building Block which represents the cash a consortium generates from each customer segment. There are two kinds of revenue streams: Transaction revenues resulting from one-time payments and recurring revenues resulting from ongoing payments to either deliver a Value Proposition to customers or provide post-purchase customer support.

A consortium must ask itself, for what value is each customer segment truly willing to pay? Successfully answering that question allows the consortium to generate one or more revenue streams from each customer segment. Each revenue stream may have different pricing mechanisms, such as fixed annual membership prices, subscription-based model, and transaction-based model. Technology companies that provide Blockchain-related professional services derive revenues from transaction fees for activity on a network, service level agreements for enterprise clients or platform fees for software-as-a-service (SaaS) contracts.

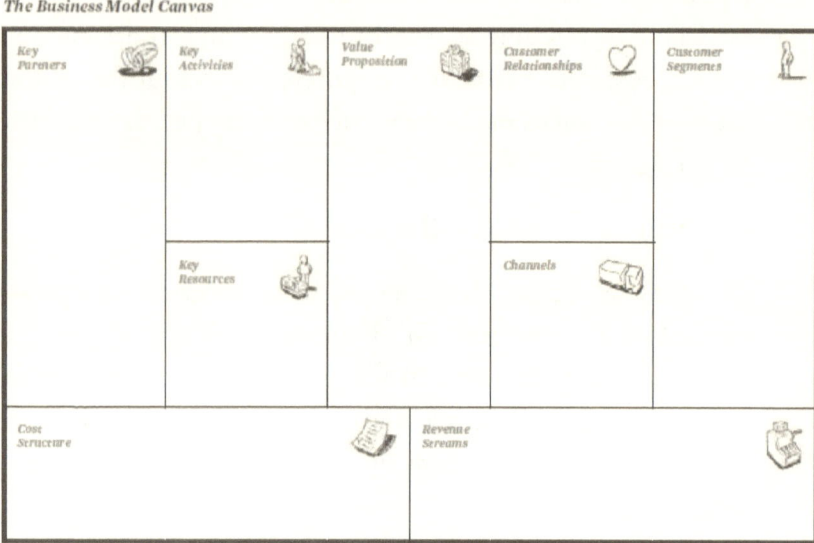

Fig 6.1 – **Business Model Canvas – Source: Alexander Osterwalder & Yves Pigneur**

6.3 Consortium Business Model Canvas

The nine blocks as we discussed earlier represent four main areas of a business: customers, offer, infrastructure and financial viability. A good consortium business model canvas should help promoters identify their resources and capability and match them to the needs in the market. It also serves as a blueprint for achieving the business strategy for the consortium. The business models allow a consortium to understand business models and their characteristics that are in existence and to position themselves appropriately. Now, with a good understanding of all the components used in business canvas, let us conceptualize a generic canvas for a Blockchain Consortium. The whole idea here, is to provide a seeding thought for the promoters of a consortium on how to design a comprehensive and well-thought out Value Proposition. Below is the generic consortium business model canvas which is just the starting the point – and not an exhaustive one. Different use cases from various business domains will have different considerations and hence it will take domain specific knowledge to build a business model.

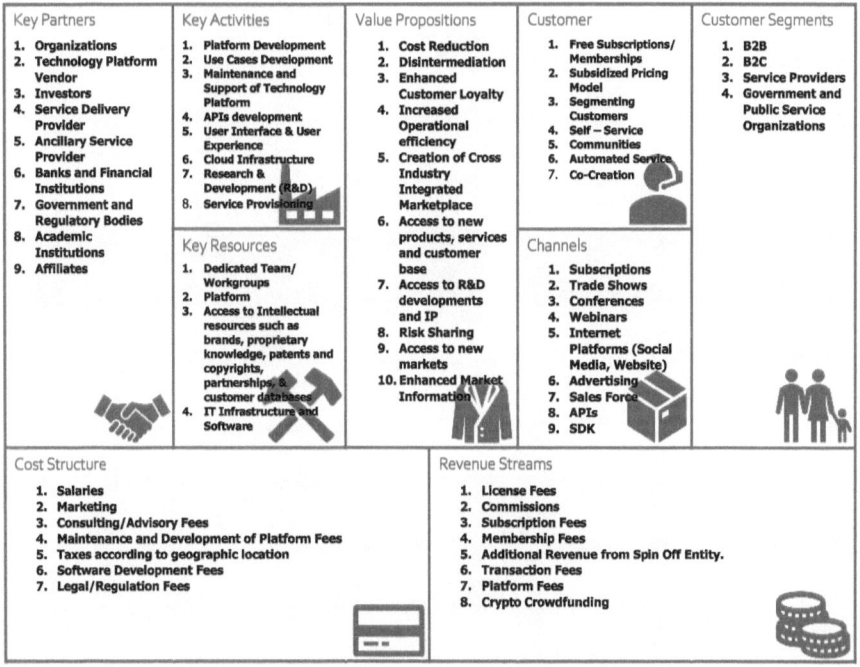

Fig 6.2 – Generic Consortium Business Model Canvas

Blockchain Consortium – Readiness Assessment Tool

As industries worldwide consider joining Blockchain Consortiums, the most important starting point to evaluate both the associated potential benefits and limitations is the mindset of whether executives are ready for the massive shift to collaborate with competitors to explore new frontiers. The Blockchain Consortium Readiness Assessment Tool is a series of important questions (not an exhaustive list) across five different dimensions for decision makers to determine their organization's readiness to join a Blockchain Consortium. The main purpose of this readiness assessment tool is to equip decision makers with a richer understanding of the opportunities and risks of Blockchain Consortiums and also improve their understanding of the requirements and elements of Blockchain Consortiums. The five dimensions are Business, Technology, Financial, Regulatory and Legal.

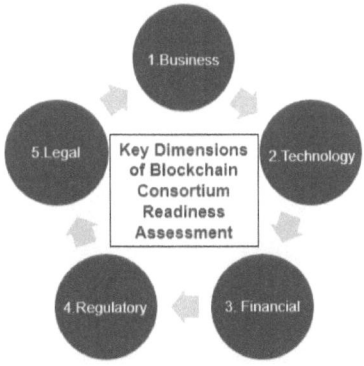

Fig 7.1 – Key Dimensions of Blockchain Consortium Readiness Assessment

Review and answer each question. Add the points associated with each question to determine your total score. There is a space in front of each question to enter a score on a scale of 1 to 5 where a score of "1" means "Strongly Disagree", and a "5" means "Strongly Agree"

(**See the scale below**). For instance, if you select "Neutral", your score will be three points for that question.

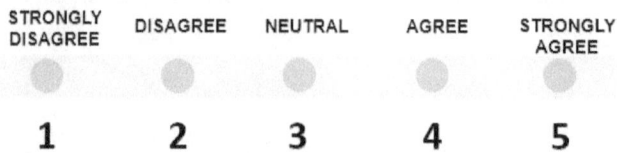

Fig 7.2 – Rating Scale for the Blockchain Consortium Readiness Assessment Tool

The total number of points will give you an insight about the readiness of your organization to join a Blockchain Consortium and help you to plan your participation accordingly. Now let's get started with the assessment and review every question under each dimension. Rate your option in the second column and enter your corresponding score in the Score column on the right.

Dimension #1: Business Considerations

Key Considerations	Rate	Score
1. You have a clear articulation of your organization's business challenges and objectives to join the Blockchain Consortium.	STRONGLY DISAGREE DISAGREE NETURAL AGREE STRONGLY AGREE 1 2 3 4 5	

2.	Your organization has a clear understanding of the Blockchain Consortium's management charter, including stakeholder case, problem and goal statements, scope, milestones, roles and responsibilities and communication plan.	STRONGLY DISAGREE 1 DISAGREE 2 NETURAL 3 AGREE 4 STRONGLY AGREE 5	
3.	Is there the need for greater trust within your organization's current business network?	STRONGLY DISAGREE 1 DISAGREE 2 NETURAL 3 AGREE 4 STRONGLY AGREE 5	

Dimension #2: Technology Considerations

	Key Considerations	Rate	Score
1.	You are confident that the consortium's Blockchain solution's underlying infrastructure will allow your organization to achieve both its business and security objectives.	STRONGLY DISAGREE 1 DISAGREE 2 NETURAL 3 AGREE 4 STRONGLY AGREE 5	
2.	You have an internal team adequately staffed with the desired cross-functionality and expertise to work on a Blockchain Implementation Project.	STRONGLY DISAGREE 1 DISAGREE 2 NETURAL 3 AGREE 4 STRONGLY AGREE 5	

Continued...

3.	Your organization has an understanding of performance-related limitations of the underlying Blockchain Consortium platform relative to the proposed Blockchain use case (e.g. transaction throughput, settlement time, and availability),	STRONGLY DISAGREE DISAGREE NETURAL AGREE STRONGLY AGREE 1 2 3 4 5	

Dimension #3: Financial Considerations

	Key Considerations	Rate	Score
1.	Does the funding model of the consortium clearly define which participating entity will fund what – and how participants will benefit from the consortium's revenues?	STRONGLY DISAGREE DISAGREE NETURAL AGREE STRONGLY AGREE 1 2 3 4 5	
2.	Your organization has done an ROI financial analysis which clearly justifies your organization's participation in the Blockchain Consortium?	STRONGLY DISAGREE DISAGREE NETURAL AGREE STRONGLY AGREE 1 2 3 4 5	

3. Your organization's auditors are able to obtain the information required from the Blockchain Consortium's management to support your financial statement disclosures.	STRONGLY DISAGREE DISAGREE NETURAL AGREE STRONGLY AGREE 1 2 3 4 5	

Dimension # 4: Regulatory Considerations

Key Considerations	Rate	Score
1. Are you aware of the factors your organization needs to consider when determining the applicability of data protection and privacy obligations?	STRONGLY DISAGREE DISAGREE NETURAL AGREE STRONGLY AGREE 1 2 3 4 5	
2. Do you know how the ownership/licensing and/or other IP rights will be dealt with in the consortium network?	STRONGLY DISAGREE DISAGREE NETURAL AGREE STRONGLY AGREE 1 2 3 4 5	
3. Does your organization have an understanding of appropriate controls across the data lifecycle (e.g. collection/creation, storage, usage, and sharing/transfer as data is shared across the Blockchain nodes) in the consortium network?	STRONGLY DISAGREE DISAGREE NETURAL AGREE STRONGLY AGREE 1 2 3 4 5	

Dimension # 5: Legal Considerations

Key Considerations	Rate	Score
1. Does your organization have an understanding of antitrust law violation risks and cross-jurisdictional regulations arising from Blockchain Consortium modes?	STRONGLY DISAGREE 1 DISAGREE 2 NETURAL 3 AGREE 4 STRONGLY AGREE 5	
2. Does your organization have an understanding of how the consortium will protect the confidentiality of its members, and what confidentiality provisions will be included within the documentation?	STRONGLY DISAGREE 1 DISAGREE 2 NETURAL 3 AGREE 4 STRONGLY AGREE 5	
3. Does your organization have an understanding on who holds legal liability in a consortium for cases such as data breach or Smart Contracts errors?	STRONGLY DISAGREE 1 DISAGREE 2 NETURAL 3 AGREE 4 STRONGLY AGREE 5	

Your total score from all the five dimensions: _____

☹ Score of 45 or below: *NOT READY FOR CONSORTIUM*

A score of 45 or below means that your organization typically represents a small ROI and limited applicability from a Blockchain Consortium approach. Consider that while the score may be low, your situation may still warrant deeper analysis as there can be a compelling reason to continue with a Blockchain approach that did not fall into the standard categorization.

☹ Score between 46 – 60: *EVALUATE AND THEN GO*

A score of between 46 and 60 means that your organization could be supported with a Blockchain approach but is not an overwhelmingly natural candidate. These situations can have powerful reasons that can still drive a Blockchain Consortium approach, yet they might also have mitigating factors that make a traditional approach a better alternative. In these situations, a more thorough analysis is typically needed.

☺ Score between 61 – 75: *READY TO GO*

A score of above 60 typically represents a compelling ROI and represents strong applicability that will benefit significantly from a Blockchain Consortium approach. It is strongly recommended that your organization consider the costs and benefits of a Blockchain approach in these instances while still considering other additive and mitigating factors internally, strategic direction, interdependencies, and related items.

Conclusion – Prepare Now, Beware of Promises and Look at the Facts

Reading up to this point, we really hope that you got a good understanding and perhaps a starting point as well, to help your organization join a Blockchain Consortium. When considering the prospect of joining or forming a consortium, companies need to evaluate how it aligns with their strategic business objectives. As described earlier, joining a Blockchain Consortium helps enterprises keep up-to-date on technology trends and competitor activity, future proof against potential new threats, and learn how to implement and integrate Blockchain. It is today's decisions that lay the foundations for the future of the company and there is no question that Blockchain will play a role in the future.

Moreover, IDC has forecast that worldwide spending on Blockchain solutions will reach nearly $4.3 billion in 2020 – a tempered 57.7% growth from the $2.7 billion spent in 2019. With this, consortiums are likely to continue to be an effective mechanism through which Blockchain-interested companies, regulators, and governments collaborate. In this landscape, the strongest consortium could become the de facto moderator of Blockchain standardization. Blockchain is still waiting for this 'break-out' moment, but with thousands of consortiums anticipated to blossom over the next few years, they are likely to play a pivotal role in Blockchain technology collaboration and commercialization.

It is these initial efforts and their related standardization, digitization, and interconnectivity that will make it possible to do even more in the future. What we should accept today is that Blockchain and consortiums are going to question conventional business models and reinvent value chains in the industry.

8.1 Factors Desirable in a Blockchain Consortium

A truly successful Blockchain Consortium is one which creates an open and neutral platform underpinned by Blockchain technology, enabling true information sharing and collaboration across value chains, thereby increasing industry innovation, reducing friction among various business entities and, ultimately, promoting more global trade. By embracing open standards and interoperability, fostering trust across the ecosystem, spurring innovation and encouraging broad-based participation, Blockchain Consortiums should usher in a new era – one in which all parties can collaborate, share data, and realize the benefits of digitization.

A successful Blockchain Consortium can be understood in three components. Each component will play a distinct role in allowing members to derive the most value for their businesses.

The Ecosystem: The foundation of any Blockchain Consortium is its business network. Each entity shares information that can be tracked, stored and actioned across the platform.

The Platform: True to its name and in the spirit of collaboration, the Blockchain Consortium platform should be accessible via an open API which helps to bring together the ecosystem through a set of open standards, and enables the sharing of information securely.

The Applications and Services Marketplace: An open Applications and Services Marketplace will allow both the consortium itself and third parties to publish fit-for-purpose services atop the consortium platform, fostering innovation and value creation.

8.1.1 Digitized Documents

A Blockchain Consortium should provide a framework for sharing documents among various participants, with security, version control, and privacy. Authorized users with the required permissions can upload, download, view and edit documents. Documents can be uploaded and shared as either structured documents, built to industry standards, which provide rich data that can be readily located, analyzed and interpreted, or unstructured documents (like scans or PDFs). The consortium's members should be permitted to access documents based on a permission matrix which can be determined through a combination of the organization's role and the document type. For e.g. Tradelens has, and is continuing to develop, standardized structured documents to replace the typical unstructured documents in use today in trade finance.

Sea Waybill	Export Declaration	Phytosanitary Certificate
Commercial Invoice	Bill of Lading	Fumigation Certificate
Packing List	Pro-Forma Invoice	Inspection Certificate
Booking Request	Arrival Notice	Certificate of Analysis
Booking Confirmation	Import Declaration	Certificate of Origin
Shipping Instructions	Health Certificate	Dangerous Goods Declaration

8.1.2 Workflow Automation

Blockchain-based solutions should provide a way for permissioned participants to immediately contribute to and extract value from the consortium ecosystem. To achieve this, the first step is for enterprises to automate legacy businesses processes which can generate numerous benefits such as completing tasks faster, providing standardization of business documents and reducing costs, to name just a few. With digitized documents and permissioned sharing, the Blockchain Consortium platform should facilitate the move away from legacy workflows (using paper or PDFs) within a single organization, to automated workflows across multiple organizations and dispense with costly, repetitive and error-prone manual inputs.

8.1.3 Application Programming Interface (API)

One of the Blockchain's strongest elements is the fact that it is guided entirely by the trust principle – interaction on the Blockchain, trusts and verifies the transaction, and relies on the agreement of all nodes to monitor what is a decentralized, otherwise untrackable operation. The API culture is equally guided by trust as a key concept. Blockchain Consortium platforms should be able to integrate seamlessly with users' in-house systems via non-proprietary, publicly available APIs that are designed specifically for ease of set-up and use. Many of the successful consortiums today use Swagger for its APIs, which is a common framework for documenting REST APIs.

8.1.4 Web User Interface (UI)

One of the most common problems with all Blockchain-based applications currently is that all the action is happening behind the scenes. It's all server side or node side. While technologies and products are still maturing, the Blockchain and server-side aspects have naturally gained more attention, both of which are vital to the project, often suggesting that there is no proper reflection in the front-end (web interface, mobile app, or UI desktop app).

To put things in context, end users of Blockchain-based solutions have no idea as to whether this particular site or mobile device is using Blockchain, which data and which steps are being coordinated on Blockchain, and what is actually going on there. Hence it's a very desirable component for Blockchain Consortium platforms to have simple yet impactful web UIs to make Blockchain applications more intuitive and accessible for consumers. A good example here would be the TradeLens consortium which developed a very easy to use and adaptable web UI for its participants. Tradelens interface can also be accessed via the web without integration. Users can also engage with essential platform features including the search and track functions and document access through a secure Single Sign On web app.

Fig 8.1 – Dubai land registry – UI Interface.

8.1.5 Standards

We believe that to encourage broad adoption and innovation, Blockchain platforms must be open and interoperable. Organizations like the Hyperledger Project of the Linux Foundation, which has hundreds of members across all sectors, have created a breeding ground for business savvy Blockchain applications. Although business applications and networks are built on different Blockchain bases such as Ethereum, Hyperledger, R3's Corda, and Ripple, eventually they must interoperate in the broader economy. Therefore, Blockchain technology requires that an enterprise establish a level of understanding that might lead to further innovations and standards. Such actions will generate unique opportunities to improve existing business practices (application of technology) and establish new business models by using Blockchain-based business networks.

8.1.6 Interoperability

The definition for Interoperability provided by the US National Institute of Standards and Technology (NIST) is: "An interoperable Blockchain architecture is a composition of distinguishable Blockchain systems, each representing a distributed data ledger, where transaction execution may span multiple Blockchain systems, and where data recorded in one Blockchain is reachable and verifiable by another possibly foreign transaction in a semantically compatible manner." One Blockchain network will simply be unable to provide all the needs for any given trade transaction. There will need to be multiple networks, each providing specific value. Data from private networks can be routed to other relevant networks for transactions without having to establish a one-to-one integration.

> "Remember that interoperability is not an individual decision, but a decision taken by at least two parties and probably more."
>
> **Henrik Jensen, Senior Blockchain Adviser, Trustworks**

From a pure business perspective, the Blockchain market will consolidate around industry consortiums, whose Blockchain network will crowd out all other networks in that space. A network of Blockchains is something more than the infrastructure that supports it. It is also a governance framework, business model, application features and middleware to interact between what the end user sees and the operation of the Blockchain. Particularly in the enterprise Blockchain space, where private networks are controlled and dominated by large powerful players, network functionality is highly specific to business needs. As a result, industry consortiums that are determined to be full-service Blockchains for their members have kind of derailed, and those that are open to interoperability with other networks, including individual networks of their members, are gaining traction.

Going forward, making interoperability a first-class citizen of Blockchains will be key to maximizing efficiencies. Interoperability here means the possibility of freely sharing values across all Blockchain networks without the need for intermediaries. In an interoperable ecosystem, you can interact with users from other Blockchain networks without spending resources on translation or experiencing downtime. You can receive information from other members, process what they send, and respond accordingly. Interoperability in Blockchain Consortium brings the following benefits:

- Smooth information sharing across participating Blockchains

- Easier execution of Smart Contracts across Blockchains

- Sharing of Blockchain solutions and cooperation on the ongoing development for enterprises

- The possibility for IT staff to develop a deep knowledge of a few prominent Blockchain standards instead of having a basic knowledge of many protocols

- Opportunity to develop partnerships within the Blockchain ecosystem

Strong interoperability would give users a much more useful, user-friendly experience. With this interoperability, users will be able to experience the seamless integration of capabilities being offered by Blockchain-based networks. To achieve interoperability from a business perspective, the following issues must be considered and addressed:

- Identity, data, and event standardization

- Governance compatibility/acceptance

- Acceptable risks

- Low switching barriers

Blockchain 3.0 projects aim for seamless interconnection between the following Blockchains:

- Multiple public Blockchains, such as Bitcoin and Ethereum

- Multiple private Blockchains, such as Hyperledger Fabric and R3

- Public and private Blockchains, such as Ethereum and Hyperledger

- Blockchains with legacy systems, such as MediLedger and SAP or Ripple and SWIFT

8.1.6.1 Blockchain Interoperability Model

The interoperability model for Blockchain solutions consists of three layers addressing the challenge for the full stack for the Blockchain solution, including the underlying Blockchain platform on which it is built.

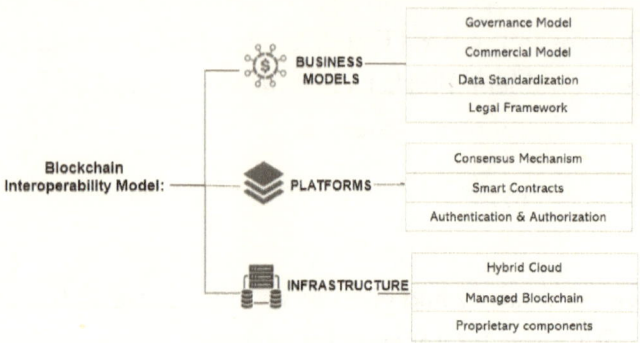

The above model is intended for organizations to structure their efforts to:

1. Clarify interoperability requirements.

2. Enable Blockchain solutions to exchange and make use of their data; and

3. Select one of three approaches to interoperability.

The three approaches unique to Blockchain interoperability as suggested by World Economic Forum (WEF) is given below. Each approach comes with pros and cons, and their usability depends on the types of systems between which one wishes to achieve interoperability; this requires organizations to be aware of all three approaches before choosing one.

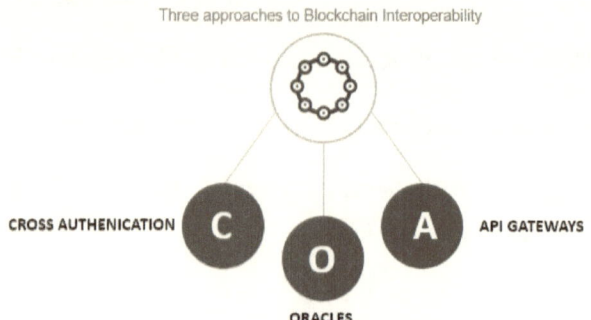

Three approaches to Blockchain Interoperability

Approach 1: Cross-authentication

Three technical methods for interoperability exist within the cross-authentication approach:

- Notary schemes

- Relays

- Hash-locking

a. **Notary Schemes**: Notary schemes are one of the simplest ways to achieve the full suite of cross-chain interoperability. However, they centralize trust, which goes against the main paradigm of Blockchain, namely decentralization. This consequence might be acceptable in situations where Blockchain Consortium members can agree on a central party to operate the notary scheme.

b. **Relays**: Relays allow each Blockchain platform to execute transactions on its own state machine using the synthetic versions of assets from the other Blockchain platform as relays allow a secure message to pass between the two platforms. For relays to work best, the Blockchain platforms should share certain characteristics, including flexible multi-signature capability and fast consensus finality.

c. **Hash-locking**: This is the most practical technical method to interoperability in cross-authentication but is also the most limiting in terms of functionality, supporting only digital asset exchange. Two general types of hash-locking exist: on-chain hashed time-lock contracts (HTLC) and off-chain hashed time-lock agreements (HTLA).

HTLCs allow for cross-chain atomic swaps and fully funded bidirectional payment channels between assets on certain types of Blockchain platforms. Unlike HTLCs, HTLA is not built as a smart contract on the Blockchain platform but an off-chain solution. Hence, it does not provide the same inbuilt decentralized characteristic as HTLC. Several companies have released interoperability solutions that are at varying levels of maturity.

Notary Schemes	Relay		Hashed Time-Lock Contract
Multi Signature **Liquid by blockstream**	QUANT AION ICON ARK BLOCKNET Polkadot	Wanchain POA Cosmos ARK Block Collider Metronome	**Contracts on-chain** BTC Relay Bitcoin Lightning Network **Agreements off-chain** R3 Corda Settler Hyperledger Quilt

Fig: Interoperability solutions released by multiple companies and mapped out according to the three technical methods presented above

Approach 2: API Gateway

An application programming interface (API) is a piece of code that governs the access point to a server and the rules developers must follow to interact with an external database, software tool or programming language. An API gateway organizes several APIs. It is the conductor that organizes the requests being processed by the underlying architecture to simplify the experience for the user, or the process of requesting for a client. Though API approach is tried and tested technology, it may not be able to guarantee data consistency across the two Blockchain platforms. Moreover, it centralizes the trust to whoever operates the APIs.

Approach 3: Oracles

An Oracle is an agent that enables the transfer of external data to the Blockchain for on-chain use. This is done using Smart Contracts that add information about real-world events to the Blockchain.

Oracles do not create actual Blockchain-to-Blockchain interoperability; they make Blockchains interoperable only with non-Blockchain systems.

To assist organizations in making decisions in interoperability approaches, the following introduces three types of systems to connect to, and four types of consortiums as the business context for interoperability needs.

	Non Blockchain Platform	Compatible Blockchain Platform	Non-Compatible Blockchain Platform
Business Financial Consortiums	Oracle	**Cross Authentication**	
	An oracle makes it possible to transfer external data to the blockchain platform for on chain use. This is done using smart contracts that add information about real world events to the blockchain platform. Once entered on the Blockchain platform, this data can be used to automate processes based on the real-world events.	Cross authentication is the only major hurdle to be resolved among compatible blockchain platforms	
Government Consortium			**API Gateways**
Business Non - Financial Consortium			When two non compatible platforms have to exchange the data, the API approach will be the last resort, which may not be able to guarantee eventual data consistency.
Technology Consortium			

Fig: Four context-dependent approaches to Blockchain interoperability

8.1.7 Convergence of Blockchain, Internet of Things (IoT) and Artificial Intelligence (AI)

The convergence of Blockchain, IoT, and AI has the potential to redefine the way businesses, industries, and even economies function, way more than they are already doing. This facilitates the sharing of information and drives more widespread adoption in different domains like Supply chain, Insurance, Autonomous Vehicle, etc. The inevitable convergence of Blockchain, IoT, and AI can form an impactful combination of security, interconnectivity, and autonomy to revolutionize the way things are done. Blockchain alone will not solve business problems. Integrated solutions will. 90%+ of Blockchain projects are weaving in other emerging technologies, especially IoT and AI.

No single organization owns the entire customer experience, and competitors and peers need to figure out how to collaborate. Blockchain, in combination with emerging technologies like IoT and AI ,will provide the way to make it happen. Once the Blockchain Consortium is in production stage, it will start working towards ecosystem extension, Interconnectivity and then Platform Enhancement. It is during the Platform Enhancement stage when the other technologies like IoT and AI will be looked into.

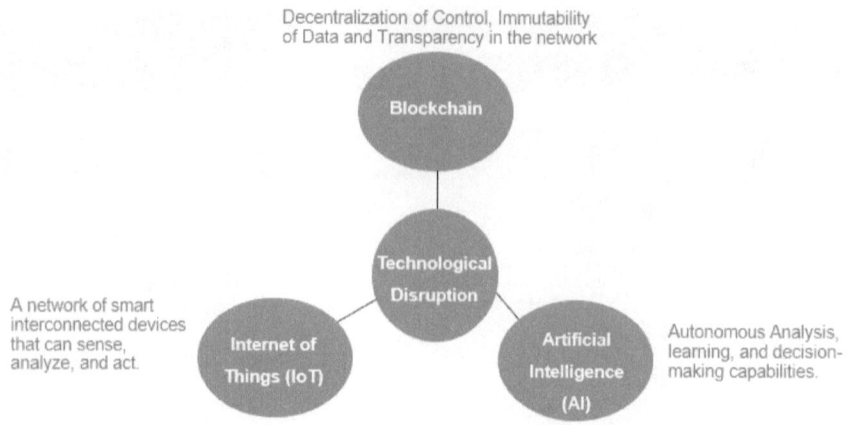

Fig: Three dimensions of Technological Disruption through convergence.

AI can be employed in large-scale Blockchain platforms to make the platforms themselves smarter. In a global, Blockchain-based supply chain platform, for example, an AI can monitor the platform to detect patterns and anomalies, potentially isolating bottlenecks or discovering safety issues faster than humans can. This could help fight fraud and increase safety, as well as help increase efficiencies and support better contingency management. Blockchain and AI could also help secure Blockchain-based financial services platforms in the AML/CFT process by tracing transactions and trying to detect AML/CFT risks.

In the real world, especially in large-scale use cases, Blockchain, AI and IoT are likely to work in concert. In a Smart City, Blockchain could be combined with IoT and AI on an infrastructure level to manage critical systems that cities depend upon, as well as improve quality of life for residents through safer and better designed urban environments.

TradeLens also uses AI, IoT, and analytics technologies to help companies move and track goods digitally across borders. Blockchain Consortiums in the insurance domain are using AI and IoT to reimagine the conventional business and operating models, spanning key functions such as underwriting, claim settlement and customer service.

8.2 Key Learnings for Future Consortium Participants

Fig 8.2 – Key Learnings for Future Consortiums

a. **Technology and Enterprise Agnosticism**

It is of utmost importance that the consortium be flexible and capable of technological interoperability. The Blockchain environment is still in its infancy, and its methods are developing rapidly, even as they are deployed. While many consortiums may align well with one particular technology and work well with it, the consortium should be flexible and fluent enough to entertain other technologies. Also, once the consortium has been formed as a legal entity, the consortium's senior leadership team should not be holding any other full-time position at an industry competitive organization. Participants in the consortium should also be diverse and represent different Blockchain protocols and technologies, as well as various industry competitors and participants. Furthermore, any technology vendor lock-in without interoperability, and potential stack integration issues where solutions are designed to operate only with one technology platform or vendor at the cost of platform flexibility, is a serious risk. To reduce this risk, it is imperative to ensure representation and participation across platforms alongside interoperability measures and universally applicable data standards.

Notably, when Blockchain Consortium working groups are formed and led by a single major player in the industry, confidence can be easily undermined and unity lost if that major player in the industry dominates the group. So, it is likely a group will organize around a dominant protocol, or even a dominant vendor. Such protocols are usually not yet flexible or interoperable. Thus far, organizations are failing to achieve recognition and buy-in from industry when organized in this way. Care must be taken in predicting how interoperability and standards operate to build robust solutions and groups.

b. **Onboarding of Regulators and Academics**

To ensure compliance with the Blockchain Consortium's activities and their using best practices for achieving the common goal, it is recommended that consortium members involve representatives from regulatory, civil, and academic bodies, especially when the group is formed by a regulated industry. Regulators should be consulted, but they do not need to be a direct member of the working community.

c. **Selection of Experienced Consortium Leader As an Independent Director**

Ideally the person appointed as consortium leader and an independent director should leave his or her current job in the industry to work exclusively on the consortium if possible and applicable. This establishes a level of market neutrality that will not be achievable if he or she remained associated with one organization in particular. The industry-wide adopted best practice of appointing a neutral independent director affords the following possibilities, which are invaluable to a new consortium:

- Provides the consortium with legitimacy both within the industry and with the Blockchain ecosystem at large

- Leverages the director's network to bring in fellow industry participants

- Provides expertise and guidance on initial use cases

d. **Role of a Neutral Convener**

Many Blockchain Consortiums in the early stages have involved a neutral convener, generally a third-party organization, to act as a glue for mobilizing collaboration among other competing organizations. For example, the MOBI consortium worked with the Media Lab at Massachusetts Institute of Technology to play this nexus role, and Energy Web partnered with the Rocky Mountain Institute. This could be particularly important during a consortium's early days, when antitrust policies are still being worked through. Earlier on also, having a 'bridge' offers a neutral meeting venue for the new group to brainstorm. However, it is not a prerequisite.

e. **Gather Critical Mass Before the Launch**

It is beneficial to gather a strong group of industry and Blockchain leaders before the consortium is officially and publicly launched. If the group is too big it won't be considered workable. There is a fine line however, and gathering critical mass along with a well-organized advertising campaign to announce the launch, is vital to creating the ecosystem 's reputation quickly. This will draw potential participants and help the project community gain real momentum.

f. **Establish a Foundational Use Case**

The committee or working group may, wherever appropriate, anchor its efforts and vision to create a POC, pilot, research study, or a standards document for an initial use case whose importance is widely recognized. This helps to test the importance and effectiveness of the initial working group and collaborative structure, provide a consistent example both externally and internally, and to guide initial focus.

g. **Develop Strong Antitrust and Governance Policies**

Legal experts and advisors should develop policies and include buy-in from the participants to ensure that they meet all needs. In addition, a review should be undertaken to determine if there are regulatory barriers that can be overcome through government permits. If so, be ready to proceed on that front.

h. **Enterprise Representatives Evangelize In-house**

Usually one or two individuals from each company will represent the organization in consortium meetings and working groups in the consortium. This person is a representative and interlocutor on behalf of that organization, representing its interests and giving importance to the working group from that organization

Top Blockchain Consortiums – Detailed Overview

1. Tradelens

TRADELENS

Name of the Consortium	TradeLens
Objective and Purpose	TradeLens is a digital platform that empowers businesses and authorities along the supply chain with a single, secure source of shipping data, enabling more efficient global trade
Website	https://www.tradelens.com
Start Date	Aug 2018
Industry Domain	Supply Chain
Blockchain Platform	Hyperledger Fabric
Members	Maersk and IBM along with other 150+ members
Entity	Joint Venture
Customer Categories	Cargo owners, ocean and inland carriers, freight forwarders, logistics providers, shippers, shipping lines, port and terminal operators, inland transportation and customs authorities

Continued...

Type of Applications	TradeLens has three key components: a business network or ecosystem comprising all members that share information about a shipment and its journey, a platform where the collaboration takes place and an applications and services marketplace where members and third parties can publish purpose-built applications and services on top of the platform
Business Model	Shippers will be paying for access to all data on shipments
Stage	Production
Future Roadmap	Not Available

2. MOBI (Mobility Open Blockchain Initiative)

Name of the Consortium	MOBI
Objective and Purpose	Promoting standards and accelerating Blockchain and DLT for mobility. Using Blockchain and related technologies to make mobility safer, greener, cheaper and more accessible
Website	https://dlt.mobi/
Start Date	May 2018
Industry Domain	Automotive
Blockchain Platform	Technology agnostic Platform
Members	85+ members which includes GM, Ford, Daimler Benz, BMW, Renault, VW, IBM, Accenture, Bosch, IOTA, and Hyperledger
Entity	Non-profit

Customer Categories	Car makers, Mobility, Energy and Infrastructure providers
Type of Applications	Vehicle Identity (VID), Usage-Based Insurance (UBI), Electric Vehicle Grid Integration (EVGI), Connected Mobility and Data Marketplace (CMDM), Finance Securitization and Smart Contracts (FSSC), Supply Chain (SC)
Business Model	A neutral community where companies openly innovate, share 'POCs' and develop standards for Blockchain in the mobility services industry
Stage	POC for Vehicle Identity (VID)
Future Roadmap	Setting common and interoperable data and technology standards and addressing notable challenges in Blockchain R&D such as protocol and application scalability and security

3. Energy Web Foundation (EWF)

Name of the Consortium	EWF
Objective and Purpose	EWF is a global, member-driven non-profit accelerating a low-carbon, customer-centric electricity system by unleashing the potential of Blockchain and decentralized technologies. EWF focuses on technology integration and development, co-creating standards and architectures, speeding adoption, and building community.
Website	https://www.energyweb.org/
Start Date	Jan 2017

Continued…

Industry Domain	Energy
Blockchain Platform	Energy Web Chain (EWChain) derived from Ethereum stack.
Members	100+ members (Founders are Rocky Mountain Institute and Grid Singularity)
Entity	Non-profit
Customer Categories	Energy Market Participants like Utilities and Grid Operators, Independent Power Producers, Global Energy Companies, Renewable Energy Developers, Corporate Energy Buyers.
Type of Applications	Energy Web Decentralized Operating System (EW-DOS), an open source stack of decentralized software and standards—including the Energy Web Chain and various SDKs.
Business Model	EW Chain features a native first-layer utility token, the Energy Web Token (EWT). Utility tokens like EWT derive value from the fact that users of a network extract economic benefits from using it and are willing to pay for those benefits. 90 million EWT will operate the EW Chain and 10 million more are used as a 10-year block validation award. The purpose of the tokens in the EWF Community Fund is to fund bounties or other activities leading to further technical development for the benefit of the Energy Web community as a whole.
Stage	Production
Future Roadmap	Cultivate an active ecosystem of affiliates, test and refine the existing features on the testnet, build additional features, test and develop a functioning decentralized on-chain governance model, refine the three software SDKs, and launch additional SDKs and tools.

4. FoodTrust

IBM Food Trust™

Name of the Consortium	Food Trust
Objective and Purpose	IBM Food Trust™, built on Blockchain, benefits all network participants with a safer, smarter, and more sustainable food ecosystem.
Website	https://www.ibm.com/in-en/Blockchain/solutions/food-trust
Start Date	August 2017
Industry Domain	Food Supply Chain
Blockchain Platform	Hyperledger Fabric
Members	100+ (Founding Members are Walmart and IBM)
Entity	Joint Venture
Customer Categories	Growers, Processors, Shippers, Retailers, Regulators, and Consumers in the food ecosystem.
Type of Applications	IBM Food Trust™ has adopted a modular approach and has built modules for the different services it is offering on the platform – Trace and Recall, Data Entry and Access, Fresh Insights and Certifications.
Business Model	The members must pay a monthly subscription fee for the subscribed modules.
Stage	Production
Future Roadmap	No Information

5. We.Trade

Name of the Consortium	We.Trade (earlier known as Digital Trade Chain)
Objective and Purpose	To provide a secure, innovative environment for banks' commercial clients engaged in import/export transactions to trade in a user-friendly and efficient way.
Website	https://we-trade.com/
Start Date	April 2018
Industry Domain	Trade Finance
Blockchain Platform	Hyperledger Fabric
Members	13 (9 Founding Banks are – Caixa Bank, Deutsche Bank, HSBC, KBC, Natixis, Nordea, Rabobank, Santander, Société Générale and UniCredit)
Entity	Not-for-Profit
Customer Categories	Companies, from SMEs to large corporates can become customers, but only through the member banks.
Type of Applications	We.Trade platform – Auto-settlement; bank payment undertaking; invoice financing
Business Model	Banks pay a yearly licence fee and per transaction fee – to onboard, maintain the platform and help build the roadmap. In order to use the platform, companies must be clients of the banks involved.
Stage	Production
Future Roadmap	Rebuild the Smart Contracts to add value-added services. Create We.Trade in Africa, Turkey, Latin-America and India and connect with We.Trade European platform.

6. Oil and Gas Consortium (OOC)

Name of the Consortium	Oil and Gas Consortium (OOC)
Objective and Purpose	Transform the Energy Industry through seamless business interactions powered by Blockchain. Building a network of business partners to create industry solution frameworks and guidelines leveraging Blockchain technology to maximize opportunities to reduce costs, improve timelines and eliminate disputes in any given process
Website	https://www.oocBlockchain.com/
Start Date	November 2018
Industry Domain	Energy
Blockchain Platform	GumboNet
Members	10 (Founding board members are Chevron, ConocoPhillips, Equinor, ExxonMobil, Hess, Pioneer Natural Resources and Repsol)
Entity	Not-for-Profit
Customer Categories	Oil and Gas Operators
Type of Applications	Truck Ticketing, AFE Balloting, JIB Exchange, Seismic Data Monitoring
Business Model	Banks pay a yearly licence fee and per transaction fee – to onboard, maintain the platform and help build the roadmap. In order to use the platform, companies have to be clients of the banks involved
Stage	POC

Continued…

Future Roadmap	Use cases identified as part of roadmap – asset tracking and traceability, asset validation, inventory management, hydrocarbon accounting, audit, billing and settlements, land lease and mineral rights management, digital letter of credit, freight bill payment and audit, and automated bill of lading validation

7. B3I – Blockchain Insurance Industry Initiative

Name of the Consortium	Blockchain Insurance Industry Initiative
Objective and Purpose	To enable the insurance market to deliver better solutions for end consumers through faster access to insurance with less administrative cost, by creating a DLT-based network through the adoption of standardized systems and protocols; through the network, enable the insurance market to optimize processes and capital allocation and generate significant cost savings
Website	https://b3i.tech/home.html
Start Date	March 2018 (This is the date of formation of B3I Services AG, the consortium initiation started in Oct 2016)
Industry Domain	Insurance
Blockchain Platform	Corda
Members	40+ (Founding members are Achmea, Aegon, Ageas, Allianz, Generali, Hannover Re, Liberty Mutual, Munich Re, SCOR, Swiss Re, Tokio Marine, XL Catlin and Zurich Insurance Group)

Entity	Partnership (For-Profit)
Customer Categories	Insurers, Brokers, Reinsurers
Type of Applications	B3I Fluidity platform. Property Catastrophe Excess of Loss (Cat XoL) Reinsurance application. Fluidity SDK to provide partners with reusable components that enable them to significantly accelerate production and deployment of their insurance applications.
Business Model	No Information
Stage	Production
Future Roadmap	Products for Commercial Insurance, Life and Health Insurance.

8. Risk Block

The Institutes·
RiskBlock Alliance

Name of the Consortium	Risk Block
Objective and Purpose	The Risk Block™ aims to create an ecosystem within the risk management and insurance industry that leverages a scalable, enterprise-level Blockchain framework to streamline the flow and verification of data in order to lower operating costs, drive efficiency from improved processes, accelerate time to market and adoption through real-world applications and impactful Blockchain use cases
Website	https://web.theinstitutes.org/riskstream-collaborative

Continued...

Start Date	December 2016
Industry Domain	Insurance
Blockchain Platform	Corda
Members	40+
Entity	Not-for-Profit
Customer Categories	Insurers, Brokers, Reinsurers
Type of Applications	Canopy Blockchain platform. Applications getting developed on the platform are: Proof of Insurance, First Notice of Loss applications.
Business Model	Royalties off of revenue generated from use of the applications built on Canopy framework by the partners.
Stage	Different use cases are at different stages.
Future Roadmap	Develop use cases related to Subrogation, Placement of Reinsurance, Life and Annuity, Commercial Certificates of Insurance, Parametric Insurance, Workers Compensation and Surety Bonds.

9. Global Shipping Business Network (GSBN)

Name of the Consortium	Global Shipping Business Network (GSBN)
Objective and Purpose	Provide a platform for all shipping supply chain participants to work collaboratively to accelerate the digital transformation of the shipping industry.

Website	https://www.cargosmart.ai/en/solutions/global-shipping-business-network/
Start Date	November 2018
Industry Domain	Supply Chain
Blockchain Platform	Oracle Blockchain Platform based on Hyperledger Fabric
Members	9 (CargoSmart with Maritime industry operator's CMA CGM, Cosco Shipping Lines, Cosco Shipping Ports, Hapag-Lloyd, Hutchison Ports, OOCL, Port of Qingdao, PSA International and Shanghai International Port Group)
Entity	Not-for-Profit (formation subject to regulatory, competition, and antitrust approvals)
Customer Categories	Carriers, terminal operators, customs agencies, shippers and logistics service providers.
Type of Applications	Use cases for digital transformation of the shipping industry. E.g. application to transform the cargo release process.
Business Model	No Information
Stage	POC conducted by CargoSmart and further development will be done through the consortium.
Future Roadmap	Develop services and applications to streamline operation processes and overall efficiency.

10. Marco Polo

Name of the Consortium	Marco Polo
Objective and Purpose	The objective of the Marco Polo Network is to facilitate interactions and create value for all its participants including financial institutions, their corporate clients, and the broader trade ecosystem
Website	https://www.marcopolo.finance/
Start Date	2017
Industry Domain	Trade Finance
Blockchain Platform	Corda
Members	30+ (Initiated by R3 and TradeIX)
Entity	For – Profit
Customer Categories	Any party that is engaged in global trade, including: buyers and sellers irrespective of size, geography or industry; banks and non-bank funders; third-party service and data providers.
Type of Applications	3 Products – payment commitment; receivables discount; payables finance
Business Model	The software and applications licence fees for the transactions executed on the network is charged to the participants of the Marco Polo Network.
Stage	Production launch planned in 2020
Future Roadmap	Option to access the Marco Polo Network via ERP-embedded App

11. Synaptic Health Alliance

Name of the Consortium	Synaptic Health Alliance
Objective and Purpose	Objective is to create a Blockchain powered platform that enables a culture of innovation, removes friction and solves the shared challenges impacting constituents across healthcare today.
Website	https://www.synaptichealthalliance.com/
Start Date	Dec 2017
Industry Domain	Insurance
Blockchain Platform	Quorum
Members	11 (Founding members are Aetna, Humana, United Healthcare, MultiPlan, Quest Diagnostics, Optum)
Entity	Joint venture
Customer Categories	Health Service Provider Organizations, Health Systems
Type of Applications	A Blockchain data exchange marketplace and application
Business Model	No Information
Stage	Pilot (Production planned in 2020)
Future Roadmap	Provide highly accurate provider Directory

12. Contour

CONTOUR

Name of the Consortium	Contour (formerly known as Voltron)
Objective and Purpose	The aim of Contour is to streamline the entire trade finance cycle by ensuring faster decision making from banks, enhancing trust, the automation of contractual agreements, and the supply chain process – by reducing the lengthy coordination of intermediaries, multiple trading partners and banks involved
Website	https://www.contour.network/
Start Date	2017
Industry Domain	Trade Finance
Blockchain Platform	Corda
Members	50+ (Initial members are BBVA, Bangkok Bank, HSBC, Natwest, ING, SEB, Scotiabank, U.S. Bancorp, Intesa Sanpaolo, Mizuho, BNP Paribas, and CTBC)
Entity	For-Profit – Standalone Legal Entity
Customer Categories	Corporates, Banks and Customers of the member banks, Importers and Exporters.
Type of Applications	Letter of Credit on Blockchain
Business Model	Contour will offer a range of pricing models depending on the module and services used by banks and corporates
Stage	Production since January 2020
Future Roadmap	Contour is set for expansion by integrating with other applications by Corda like KYC and payments so that Contour users will benefit end-to-end, i.e. from onboarding the customer to delivery and payment of goods – via a single platform

13. Komgo

Name of the Consortium	Komgo SA
Objective and Purpose	Komgo's mission is to catalyze the commodity trade network by providing a fully decentralized, interoperable Blockchain solution to act as a data exchange for the industry
Website	https://komgo.io/
Start Date	2018
Industry Domain	Trade Finance
Blockchain Platform	Quorum
Members	17 Banks and 120+ Corporates (Founding members are ABN AMRO, BNP Paribas, Citi, Crédit Agricole Group, Gunvor, ING, Koch Supply & Trading, Macquarie, Mercuria, MUFG Bank, Natixis, Rabobank, Shell, SGS and Société Générale)
Entity	For-Profit
Customer Categories	Banks, Commodity Traders, Insurers, Manufacturers
Type of Applications	Products for KYC; Tracking of documents; Letter of Credit and Standby Letter of Credit
Business Model	Subscription service based on the number of users and number of legal entities.
Stage	Production since 2018
Future Roadmap	Digital trade finance related products (receivables discounting and inventory financing), streamlining trade finance (Konsole), optimizing liquidity and managing risk (Market)

14. eTradeConnect

Name of the Consortium	eTrade Connect
Objective and Purpose	To facilitate the settlement and financing of trades through the sharing of trade data, ensuring high security, and efficiency in an effective and cost-efficient way
Website	https://www.etradeconnect.net/Portal
Start Date	Oct 2017
Industry Domain	Trade Finance
Blockchain Platform	Hyperledger Fabric
Members	12
Entity	Not-for-Profit consortium managed by the Hong Kong Monetary Authority
Customer Categories	Banks, Logistic Service Providers, Buyers and Sellers.
Type of Applications	A DLT-based platform where customers and their trading partners can conduct trades and trade financing
Business Model	No Information
Stage	Production
Future Roadmap	Link eTradeConnect with platforms from other regions in order to enable cross-border trade financing like We.Trade, GSBN and integration with Corporate Procurement System through "ERP Connect" by PwC

15. MineHub

MINEHUB

Name of the Consortium	MineHub
Objective and Purpose	MineHub modernizes the mining and metals supply chain, leading to greater transparency and traceability via real-time tracking, automation, streamlined credit management, paperless transactions, and greater business intelligence.
Website	https://minehub.com
Start Date	Jan 2018
Industry Domain	Mining Supply chain
Blockchain Platform	Hyperledger Fabric
Members	MineHub has been working in collaboration with its consortium members IBM and other industry participants, including ING Group, Wheaton Precious Metals, Ocean Partners, Kutcho Copper, Capstone Mining and White and Case to develop the platform.
Entity	For-Profit
Customer Categories	Miners, smelters, surveyors, insurance providers, ports and warehouses, shipping and banks.
Type of Applications	Minehub platform with solution for Supply chain, Contract Management, Credit Management, Invoice and Payments and Insights.
Business Model	The revenues are based on recurring annual subscription fees from both, members and parties outside the consortium.
Stage	Production
Future Roadmap	Digitize the complete Mining Supply Chain business. Currently, the first release enables miners to capture mineral production and digital contracts with buyers.

16. Financial Blockchain Shenzhen Consortium

FISCO 金链盟

Name of the Consortium	Financial Blockchain Shenzhen Consortium (FISCO)
Objective and Purpose	FISCO strives to integrate and coordinate research resources to advance financial Blockchain technology, as well as promote synergy and collaboration for Blockchain-based financial application research. With these establishments, it seeks to facilitate the members' R&D capabilities to apply financial consortium Blockchain in business scenarios
Website	https://www.fisco.com.cn/indexEN.html
Start Date	May 2016
Industry Domain	Finance
Blockchain Platform	FISCO – BCOS based on Ethereum
Members	110+
Entity	Non-Profit
Customer Categories	Banking, Fund management, Securities brokerage, Insurance, Regional equity exchanges, and Financial information service companies
Type of Applications	FISCO Blockchain open source platform
Business Model	No information
Stage	Production
Future Roadmap	Projects in the financial areas of credit, equity, loyalty points system, insurance, commercial bills, Cloud service, digital assets, and wealth management issuance and trading on FISCO Blockchain platform

17. India Trade Connect

Name of the Consortium	India Trade Connect
Objective and Purpose	Domestic trade finance Blockchain-based network, enabling automation and transparency, and improving risk mitigation in domestic trade and supply chain finance operations.
Website	https://www.edgeverve.com/finacle/casestudy/india-trade-connect/
Start Date	March 2017
Industry Domain	Trade Finance
Blockchain Platform	Finacle Trade Connect, which is built on the principle of permissioned networks, is agnostic to the underlying DLT and is certified to work on most major platforms including R3's Corda, Hyperledger Fabric, and Ethereum stacks.
Members	Edgeverve (an Infosys company) along with seven Banks ICICI Bank, Axis Bank, IndusInd Bank, RBL Bank, Yes Bank, Kotak Bank, South Indian Bank.
Entity	Joint Venture
Customer Categories	Bank, Sellers, Buyers, Logistics and Insurance providers.
Type of Applications	Comprehensive set of end-to-end trade products and functions including Open Account, Letter of Credit, Bank Guarantee, Bill collection, C2C and B2C transactions.
Business Model	No information
Stage	Production
Future Roadmap	Enhance Trade Connect with AI and machine learning.

18. PharmaLedger

Name of the Consortium	PharmaLedger
Objective and Purpose	The Pharma Ledger consortium will create a scalable Blockchain platform validated through reference use cases in supply chain, clinical trials and health data that will serve trendsetters in the industry, thus enabling early adopters.
Website	https://pharmaledger.eu/
Start Date	January 2020
Industry Domain	Healthcare
Blockchain Platform	The platform under design is planned to support multiple chains with the aim of using the Blockchain protocol, which is deemed to most fit the use case.
Members	29 Members (including 12 pharmaceutical companies and 17 others – a mix of technology firms, hospitals, universities, research organizations, healthcare providers and patient representatives)
Entity	Joint Venture
Customer Categories	Pharma Companies, Hospitals, Healthcare Providers
Type of Applications	The platform will be interoperable and plans to use APIs to integrate with a Blockchain, so the application layer is relatively Blockchain agnostic.
Business Model	No information available

Stage	POC
Future Roadmap	The following use cases in three industry domains such as supply chains, health data, and clinical trials are planned for the future – Clinical supply (traceability), Finished goods traceability, Anti-counterfeiting, Personalized medicines, Dynamic permissioning, eConsent, IoT medical device trials, Clinical trials recruitment.

ANNEXURE – (B)

List of other Consortiums

1. GLBC Global Legal Blockchain Consortium
https://legalconsortium.org/

The Global Legal Blockchain Consortium formed in 2017, comprises over 300 large companies, law firms, software companies, and universities that have joined together to develop standards to govern the use of Blockchain technology in the business of law. The mission of the Global Legal Blockchain Consortium is to enhance the security, privacy, productivity, and interoperability of the legal technology ecosystem.

Specifically, the consortium is focused on:

- Data integrity and authenticity for contracts, documents, and similar data.

- Data privacy and security for contracts, documents, and communications.

- Interoperability between large corporate legal departments and law firms.

- Productivity improvements and cost savings in the operation of legal departments and law firms.

- Use of Blockchain to fortify and augment existing legal technology investments adding important functionality to legacy systems to extend their useful life.

2. CULegder: https://www.culedger.com/

CULedger's goal is to deliver a trusted peer-to-peer services network of verifiable exchange for financial cooperatives. It is a credit union owned CUSO (credit union service organization) that is creating the premier platform of digital exchange for financial cooperatives globally. In working through a national consortium made up of credit unions and trusted industry investors, CULedger has pioneered new developments related to global self-sovereign decentralized identity, MemberPassTM, that will further enhance the trust credit unions have with their members. CULedger provides advantages to credit unions and their members by

a. reducing risks associated with cybersecurity and fraud,

b. improving member experience,

c. streamlining internal processes and

d. reducing administrative and operational costs.

By creating a Permissioned Blockchain network where services can be shared among all credit unions, CULedger claims to improve services such as identification authentication, regulatory compliance around KYC, lending and payments, while making it easier and more efficient for consumers to conduct any interactions that require authentication. And, all future applications, including those in CULedger's current roadmap such as loan participations and cross-border payments, will be enabled through a private, permissioned distributed ledger network (i.e. only selecting entry of authentic and verified participants) – development for which is in progress

3. Decentralized Identity Foundation (DIF) – https://identity.foundation/

DIF, a non-profit entity was formed in May 2017 as an engineering-driven consortium focused on developing the foundational elements necessary to establish an open ecosystem for decentralized identity and ensure interoperability between all participants. DIF vision is to enable a world where decentralized identity solutions allow entities to gain control over their identities and allow trusted interactions. The foundation, with around 100 members currently, is encouraging an implementation-led approach based on open source code contributions to develop an interoperable identity stack which can be used and adopted without restrictions. Also, it closely collaborates with standardization bodies and organizations like IETF, W3C, W3C CCG, Hyperledger, Trust over IP etc.to ensure that more matured concepts or specifications and standards can be formalized. Given below are different working groups scoped by functional areas, driving the standard specifications backed by open source code.

a. Identifiers and Discovery

b. Authentication

c. Claims and Credentials

d. Side tree Development and Operating Group

e. Secure Data Storage

4. Integrated Engineering Blockchain Consortium (IEBC) – https://iebc.co/

IEBC is a global consortium of integrated engineering innovations applied to the sustainability of worthy enterprises. IEBC's goal is to reduce systemic risk in the world. IEBC is developing a decentralized platform for Engineering, Finance, and Insurance protocols. The consortium is developing a native Blockchain platform CoEngineers.io – a novel application of Blockchain technology, game mechanics, and two stable cryptographic tokens that serve to measure intangible assets into tangible existence.

CoEngineers is a publishing platform for engineers. It measures the true impact of engineers upon the economy, society, and environment. The fundamental building block of CoEngineers is a network of claims and validations related to the physical state of the world expressed as a function of time and space. The utility of this project is to provide three classes of data related to the physical state:

a. Identification of risk exposures.

b. Probability that risk exposure may happen.

c. Assessment of consequences in the event that risk exposures manifest.

This is accomplished by recording the day-to-day claims and validations made by engineers.

The CoEngineers platform provides several functions:

a. A decentralized ledger upon which the statements of physical fact may be verified, validated and recorded.

b. A time-function upon which to synchronize, identify, and revise physical state.

c. A multi-agent algorithmic game

5. Retail Blockchain Consortium (RBC) – https://www.retailBlockchainconsortium.org/

The RBC is a global collaboration led by Oracle, UCL CBT and MonoChain, and involves leading retailers, universities, technology companies, Blockchain companies and service providers. RBC was launched in Jan 2019 as a not-for-profit organization with a goal to advance the usage of DLT within the Retail industry. The RBC explores and advances the usage of DLT within the retail value chain. The consortium will provide open resource tools and specifications for academic and commercial partners to leverage this innovative transformational technology for specific retail value chain use cases.

The consortium has four working groups: Grocery Supply chain, Fashion and Circular Economy, Pharmaceutical Supply Chain, B2B Supply Chain. The membership is invite-only open to individuals and organizations around the globe operating in Retail and Supply Chain space.

6. Tracr – https://www.tracr.com/

Tracr™, the end-to-end Diamond Industry Blockchain traceability platform is developed by the De Beers Group in collaboration with key industry stakeholders (currently 30+ members), such as diamond producers, trade associations, graders, governments, logistics providers, retailers, and banks. It connects the Diamond Industry by establishing Provenance, Authenticity and Traceability throughout the entire value chain.

Tracr goals are:

a. to provide a reliable record of a diamond's origin

b. to verify if it is a natural stone

c. to make it traceable throughout the pipeline

Industry players can join in by going through a KYC process and integrating with the Blockchain. They create an identity and then start uploading data about their diamonds.

7. Clipeum

Clipeum is a consortium led by Société Générale and 12 European financial institutions including BPCE/Natixis, Credit Agricole, Commerzbank, Allianz, Banque Postale, BpiFrance, Euler Hermes, Tikehau and UniCredit. It is a KYC platform (set to go live later in 2020) based on a distributed registry technology built on R3 Corda with an aim to build a European KYC network with the clients at the centre, having full control over data sharing and access permissions.

The principle of Clipeum is that every enterprise has a vault in which they store their KYC information. Financial institutions can request access to that information and, if the corporate approves the request, the information and all of its updates are made available to the financial institution until the access right is revoked.

8. BankChain – https://www.bankchaintech.com/

BankChain is a community of banks for exploring, building, and implementing Blockchain solutions. The consortium was formed in February 2017 and now has 37 members and 22 live projects. Some of BankChain's projects include: Global marketplace for Invoice discounting, Charge Registry, Corporate KYC, Document authentication and verification using Electronic signatures, Issuance, storage and distribution of Trade Documents, Transparent rating and review, Global marketplace for Government Securities, and global marketplace for private Debt Instruments.

9. Bay Area Trade Finance Blockchain Platform (BATFB)

The BATFB is a DLT-based platform that was unveiled by the People's Bank of China in September 2018. The platform, which now incorporates more than 28 banks in Shenzhen, has processed over $4.5 billion worth of foreign exchange transactions to date. The intended purpose of the project has been real-time traceability, the elimination of fraud, and a reduction in the need for manual transactions. The main purpose of the project is to expand the availability of trade finance to SMEs and reduce the trade friction as Hong Kong and Macau are subject to capital controls. The platform, which is built using proprietary technology, has announced plans to link with Hong Kong, China-based platform eTrade Connect, which is powered by Hyperledger Fabric.

The first phase is focused on trade finance for suppliers, and later, it plans to explore Letters of Credit and guarantees.

10. Global Trade Connectivity Network – www.mas.gov.sg/development/fintech/trade-finance

The Global Trade Connectivity Network (GTCN) is a collaboration between the Monetary Authority of Singapore (MAS) and the Hong Kong Monetary Authority (HKMA) to develop a DLT infrastructure for cross-border transactions. The initiative strikes out to reduce the number of pain points involved in traditional trade finance transactions, leveraging DLT to build infrastructure for more efficient cross-border trade and trade finance transactions. The GTCN has since been built on open architecture so that it will be a seamless process for other jurisdictions beyond just MAS and HKMA to join. GTCN will provide a common view for trade finance applications between Singapore and Hong Kong, empowering participating banks to share immutable and auditable ledgers across the border, while maintaining data privacy and confidentiality through a distributed network.

Listed below are the key benefits of GTCN:

a. Mitigation of Duplicate Invoice Financing

b. End-to-end Digitalization of Trade Finance

c. Increased interoperability across platforms

11. Fnality – https://www.fnality.org/

Fnality International (Fnality) is a consortium initiative led by 14 global banks that was founded in May 2019. The project was initially called Utility Settlement Coin, started by Swiss bank UBS and supported by 13 other global banks. Before Fnality, the USC Project focused on finding a more efficient means of international cross-border payments in a future world of tokenized wholesale markets. Building on this base, the focus for Fnality from May 2019 is to create and deploy a solution that satisfies all the legal, regulatory, operational, and technical aspects of a Distributed

Financial Market Infrastructure (dFMI). Fnality was born out of the need to transform clearing and settlement processes, enable Delivery vs. Payment (DvP) in tokenized securities markets, and, in the secured funding market, enable instant settlement on a Payment vs. Payment (PvP) basis. Fnality is built using Clearmatics' Blockchain architecture which is a private version of Ethereum called Autonity.

12. DELIVER

In 2018, Dutch bank ABN AMRO collaborated with the Port of Rotterdam and Samsung SDS on a Blockchain trade initiative, DELIVER.

DELIVER supports cross-supply chain end-to-end visibility for multi-modal cargo transport via ocean carrier, truck and inland barge shipping, as well as streamlining access to finance.

The Blockchain logistics platform is built for interoperability between different Blockchain technologies, including Samsung's Nexledger, Hyperledger Fabric, Ethereum and potentially others. Samsung SDS is also planning for supporting apps developed with various Blockchain platforms, such as EOS, through technology development in the future.

This interoperability platform aims to be the foundation of a global logistics network.

By connecting different platforms, Deliver supports a number of functions such as document notarization, double payment prevention, and asset transfer. The group announced they have successfully tracked and instantly financed a shipping container and the POC phase is complete.

13. Blockchain Interoperability Alliance (BIA)

At the end of 2017, the BIA was formed to establish links between independent Blockchain networks. It was created by Wanchain, AION, and ICON with the goal of advancing standards that would foster a greater degree of connectivity between disparate Blockchains, address the issue of scalability, and establish best practices for inter-chain communication within the industry.

This alliance will focus on developing a common set of standards for Blockchain interoperability to ensure the shared vision of a global ecosystem of connected Blockchains is achieved. The alliance's first priority is to share and collaborate on research and design for cross-chain transactions and communication.

14. The Coupon Bureau (https://www.thecouponbureau.org/)

The Coupon Bureau (TCB) which was started in 2016 is an open-market platform connecting all stakeholders to the new Universal Positive Offer File. This helps support secure promotions and enable the ongoing growth of the industry. This allows all current stakeholders to maintain their current business functions and expand those by utilizing Positive Offer File connectivity.

Mission: The mission of TCB is to connect manufacturers, retailers and consumers through technology and community. This will be achieved by developing new technology, by supporting third party technologists, by deploying educational programs for industry stakeholders, and by giving back to the community.

TCB is a non-profit corporation that owns The Coupon Bureau technology and is led by an industry representative Board of Governors. This leadership protects the mission and vision of the organization. TCB's day-to-day activities are led by an Executive Director, the non-profit's CEO, who directs the TCB team as they work together to execute the requirements necessary to complete the goals, tasks and vision of the board. Technology roadmaps, organizational planning, financial planning and charitable planning take place at the board level, and are carried out by the TCB staff.

TCB is using the Hedera Consensus Service (HCS) from Hedera Hashgraph to provide a real-time, tamper-proof log for all coupon events on its platform. This will allow coupon providers, manufacturers, clearinghouses, and retailers the ability to validate in real-time when coupons are registered and redeemed on the platform, without having to trust any single party.

15. Trusted IoT Alliance (https://www.iiconsortium.org/)

Trusted IoT Alliance (TIoTA) is an open software consortium created in 2017 to support the creation of a secure, scalable, interoperable, and trusted IoT ecosystem. The core concept behind TIoTA is to leverage software advances in cryptography, DLT, secure enclaves and other state-of-the-art-approaches to ensure fast and secure trust-building at an unprecedented scale and speed. TIoTA's members span hardware communications, payment, logistics, and numerous other tech sectors.

The mission of the Trusted IoT Alliance is to bring companies together to develop and set the standard for an open source Blockchain protocol to support IoT technology in major industries worldwide. Its membership is focused on 'working together to advance IoT and Blockchain' by leading pilots, publishing open source code, and coordinating standards and reference architecture.

The alliance is Blockchain agnostic and will support integration across any open source enterprise Blockchain or DLT platform that has the potential to become a backend for widespread commercial and industrial adoption. The alliance aims to foster interoperability and interworking across Blockchain platforms, applications, and in doing so remove barriers to broad scale adoption of Blockchain technology.

In Jan 2020, the Industrial Internet Consortium (IIC) and the Trusted IoT Alliance (TIoTA) announced they are combining memberships to drive industry collaboration. Members of the two organizations will now work under the IIC to research.

Project Ubin Sets the Bar for Central Banks Looking to Adopt Blockchain

Six months after the Bank for International Settlements' proclamation that over 80% of central banks contemplate Blockchain to issue digital currencies, we take a look at how things have fallen into place. CBDCs – an abbreviation for Central Bank Digital Currencies – have stepped into the limelight with their promise of increased security, efficiency and resilience. This means two things: 1) Traditional financial systems are at the end of their technological life cycle, and 2) Disruption is slowly being embraced even amongst the most conservative of industries. But what comes after the initial burst of animation?

Enter Project Ubin. A multi-year project started sometime back in 2016 by the Monetary Authority of Singapore (MAS is Singapore's Central Bank), in collaboration with selected industry partners, the initiative recently celebrated the successful completion of Phase 5. To put this into perspective:

- Phase 1 & 2: Tokenized SGD and re-imagined RTGS (Real-Time Gross Settlements) on Blockchain

- Phase 3 & 4: Enabled interoperability of Blockchain-based networks for DvP and cross-border PvP

- Phase 5: Launched production ready "Ubin V", a domestic multi-currency payments that can be implemented for international settlement

Project Ubin starts off grounded in practical value, while still holding an ambitious mission to realize the full potential of CBDC. The basic mission reads: to explore the use of Blockchain and DLT for clearing and settlement of payments and securities. It adds: This is with the eventual goal of developing simpler to use and more efficient alternatives to today's [financial] systems based on central bank issued digital tokens.

These words, not merely a cursory nod to the possibilities of Blockchain or DLT, are a refreshing illumination of how central banks can hope to truly appreciate the technology when approached with considerate, thoughtful planning. Tracing the trajectory of the project from beginning to end, it is clear that each breakthrough builds upon its predecessor, discouraging the spiel of progress for the sake of progress. Case in point: While Phase 5 has concluded, Ubin V continues to undergo industry testing with more than 40 financial and non-financial firms, to determine its ability to integrate with commercial Blockchain applications.

Project Ubin In a Nutshell – Things You Would Like to Know About Ubin

- The Ubin V network was designed with principles of open architecture, open connectivity and interoperability to enable ease of integration across these networks for seamless, end-to-end processing.

- The Ubin payments network uses J.P. Morgan's Quorum Blockchain protocol as the base infrastructure, coupled with the network and application capabilities developed as part of the

IIN and JPM Coin product, and provides API connectivity to interfacing applications.

- Successfully identified 124 Blockchain use cases, highlighting 16 in capital markets, trade and supply chain finance, insurance, and beyond financial services. (Refer to the list of use cases along with the chosen industry partner below).

- The five key features in the Ubin payments network are issuance, transfer, redemption, conditional payments and reconciliation.

- Ubin V supports wholesale inter-bank and corporate payments and was developed and tested with SGD and USD currencies with the intention of working with other central and commercial banks to include other currencies.

Summary of use cases developed and tested in Project Ubin.

Industry Focus Area	Area	Use Case Description	Industry Partner
Capital Markets	Private Equities	Private exchange to facilitate trading of equities in privately held companies	1X.EXCHANGE
	Private Equities	Platform for issuance, custody and trading of digital securities	iSTOX
	Bonds	Trading and settlement platform for issuance and lifecycle management of digital securities	STACS Blockchain for Finance
	Syndicated Loans	Primary syndication and secondary trading of syndicated loans	iLex IHS Markit

Continued...

	Multi-Stage Investments & Disbursements	Infrastructure assets funding in a low-cost and secure manner	ALL INFRA
	Cross-border Settlement	Cross-border securities settlement and dividend payments using digital currencies	SYGNUM
Insurance	Health care Insurance	Lifecycle management of healthcare insurance claims	Digital Asset
	Automobile Insurance	Sharing & recording of information across participants for automobile insurance claims	Inmediate
Trade and Supply Chain Finance	Supply Chain Digitalization	Procure-to-Pay platform for exchanges of trade documents, with automated document verification and payment processing	DIGITAL VENTURES
	Supply Chain Digitalization	Unified platform to connect buyers and sellers for orders, logistics and payments	INVICTUS
	Supply Chain Digitalization	Exchange, verification and automatic matching of trade data to obtain digital payment obligations	MarcoPolo
	Supply Chain Digitalization	Electronic matching of trade data for bank payment obligation transactions	ess DOCS

	Supply Chain Financing	Supply chain financing for SMEs with non-bank institutional capital	Crediti
Beyond Financial Services	Media & Advertising	Streamlining digital supply chain of programmatic advertising	Aqilliz
	Salary Payments	HR payments solution for real-time, accurate salary payments for gig workers and organizations	octomate Adecco

Interoperability Examples

Given the importance of Blockchain interoperability, there are several initiatives currently being developed across different platforms. Some of the significant examples are given below :

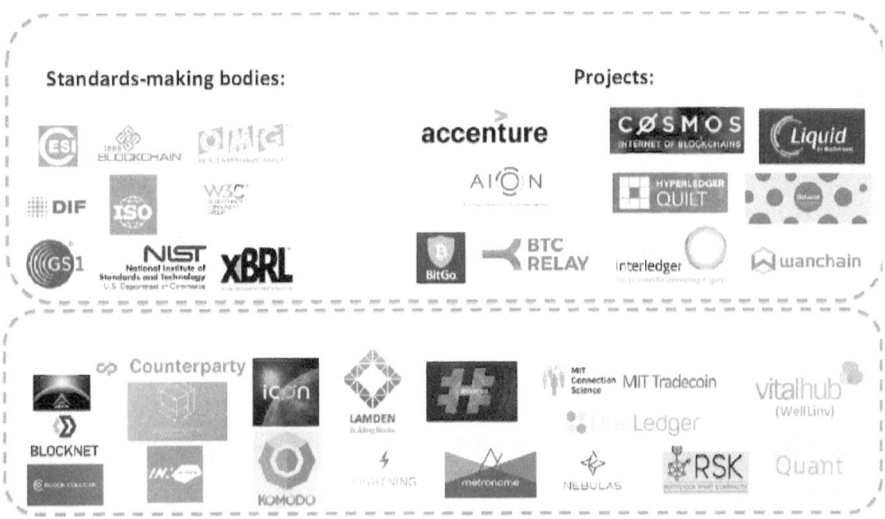

Fig: Blockchain Interoperability Current Landscape

1. **Deloitte** has connected Hyperledger Fabric and Ethereum with Singapore Exchange (SGX) and MAS, the Central Bank of Singapore. The main objectives of this project undertaken by Deliotte were to:

   a. reduce the turnaround time of the DvP process from T+2 to T+0

b. lower the risk of counterparties

c. reduce the liquidity required in the ecosystem

The delivery leg – i.e. the transfer of title of the securities – was executed on the permissioned Hyperledger Fabric, while the payment leg using the CBDC named Ubin, each coin backed with one SGD, was running on crypto-enabled Ethereum. Both Fabric and Ethereum are open-sourced and widely adopted and are most suitable for delivery and payment respectively. The challenge was how to integrate these two Blockchain technologies together.

2. **DELIVER** is a Blockchain trade platform developed by Samsung SDS in collaboration with Dutch bank ABN AMRO and the port of Rotterdam. The platform is built for interoperability between different Blockchain technologies, including Samsung's Nexledger, Hyperledger Fabric, Ethereum and other potentials. Samsung SDS is also planning for supporting apps developed with various Blockchain platforms such as EOS, through technology development in the future.

3. **Cosmos** is currently one of the biggest names among Blockchain interoperability initiatives. It runs on the Tendermint Byzantine fault tolerance protocol. Independent Blockchains, referred to as zones, are plugged into the Cosmos network. Zones are all connected to the Cosmos Hub and can interact with each other. New zones can connect to the network and exchange value, thanks to the standardized protocol. One distinguishing feature of Cosmos is granting zones the freedom to preserve their consensus mechanism.

4. **Polkadot**: The idea of Polkadot is attributed to Gavin Wood, one of Ethereum's founders. The distinguishing characteristic of Polkadot is that it facilitates not only transactions but also data exchange. The Polkadot ecosystem contains parachains (individual Blockchains that became part of the Polkadot environment),

and a relay chain that is a central connector between parachains. Each parachain can have different characteristics and spread its transactions across the ecosystem. All chains that become a part of the Polkadot ecosystem are required to abandon their consensus mechanism to the Polkadot's mechanism, but they have the freedom of developing the structure and function of their Blockchain.

5. **Aion**: Aion was developed by Nuco, a Canadian company specializing in enterprise Blockchain solutions. Aion is very similar to its competition as it allows different Blockchains to exchange value eliminating the intermediary. However, Aion distinguishes itself by working toward integrating AI in its consensus model. Most Blockchain systems are not able to accommodate large amounts of data. Aion addresses this issue by using a high-performance virtual machine and a scalable database.

6. **Ark**: This is one of the most ambitious projects in Blockchain interoperability with a big community of supporters. Ark aims to create a Blockchain interoperability solution that is scalable and adaptable. Therefore, Ark automated the creation of new Blockchains within the ecosystem. As a result, users can create new Blockchains within minutes. Ark has built-in support for numerous programming languages including Java, Swift, Python, and Ruby. This makes Ark accessible to people who prefer working with particular languages.

7. **Quant Network** aims to foster interoperability through its native Blockchain software Overledger. Overledger facilitates access across different Blockchain networks. This allows the creation of multi-application chains (MApps) that can leverage the functionalities of different Blockchains. For example, developers can pick a particular feature of one Blockchain, such as high throughput, and couple it with a feature derived from another Blockchain, such as decentralization. This is done to optimize the

agnostics (the ability of one Blockchain to interact with another) of the application. Overledger is designed to be future proof, which it accomplishes by isolating the transaction layers between Blockchains. Indeed, this is a core feature of Overledger; it is a protocol that runs on top of other Blockchains rather than being a Blockchain itself.

8. **Wanchain**, also a founding member of Blockchain Ineroperability Alliance (BIA), is focused on providing access to all digital assets on disparate Blockchain networks, similar to banks offering access to a variety of fiat currencies. Wanchain aims to unite siloed Blockchain structures through the use of cross-chain Smart Contracts, essentially being a middleware that facilitates transactions between Blockchains.

Like most of the other projects dedicated to interoperability, Wanchain uses a Proof of Stake (POS) consensus mechanism. A core differentiator — Wanchain utilizes three functional modules: a registration module, a cross-chain transaction data transmission module, and a transaction status query module.

9. **Komodo** is a dynamic Blockchain protocol that facilitates interconnectivity between Blockchain networks as well as their native communities. Komodo is a multi-chain platform that allows developers and projects to create a customizable, dedicated Blockchain with completely independent infrastructure and smart-contract functionality. All projects or Blockchains under the Komodo ecosystem are equipped with support for atomic swaps and cross-chain Smart Contracts that facilitate interoperability. Komodo uses a delayed POW (dPOW) consensus mechanism, leveraging on the security strength of the Bitcoin network.

References

1. Why Consortiums Matter – https://www.investopedia.com/terms/c/consortium.asp

2. Blockchain Consortium – https://101Blockchains.com/Blockchain-consortium/

3. So, you've decided to join a Blockchain Consortium – Deloitte – https://www2.deloitte.com/content/dam/Deloitte/us/Documents/technology/us-cons-Blockchain-consortium.pdf

4. Emergence of Blockchain Consortiums – Deloitte – https://www2.deloitte.com/us/en/insights/focus/signals-for-strategists/emergence-of-Blockchain-consortiums.html

5. WEF Blockchain Toolkit – https://widgets.weforum.org/Blockchain-toolkit/modules/

6. Blockchain Governance Models Insights for Enterprises.-BCoE 2019-02- University of Arkansas – Mary Lacity, Zach Steelman, Paul Cronan – https://cpb-us-e1.wpmucdn.com/wordpressua.uark.edu/dist/5/444/files/2019/11/BCCoEWhitePaper022019OPEN.pdf

7. Deloitte Global Blockhain Survey 2019 – https://www2.deloitte.com/content/dam/Deloitte/se/Documents/risk/DI_2019-global-Blockchain-survey.pdf

8. Top Four Enterprise Blockchain Consortiums Trends – 2019 – ESG Intelligence – https://esg-intelligence.com/Blockchain-articles/2019/06/19/top-four-enterprise-Blockchain-consortiums-trends-2019/

9. Dubai launches Blockchain Know Your Customer consortium – Ledger Insight – https://www.ledgerinsights.com/dubai-Blockchain-kyc-know-your-customer-consortium/

10. MOBI's First Standard Released on Vehicle Identity https://medium.com/@dlt_mobi/mobis-first-standard-released-on-vehicle-identity-44cc36d1083c

11. Friedman, Lynette and LeBan, Karen. 2014. Consortium Management and Leadership Training Facilitator's Guide. CORE Group: Washington D.C.

12. Arun, Jai Singh, Nitin Gaur, Jerry et al. *Blockchain for Business: Discover How Blockchain Networks Are Transforming Companies, Driving Growth, and Creating New Business Models.* Pearson Education., 2019.

13. Radcliffe, M. (2019). Consortium Blockchain governance: four critical issues for enterprise Blockchain projects. https://www.dlapiper.com/en/us/insights/publications/2019/08/Blockchain-governancekey-issues-in-governance-for-Blockchain-consortium-2019/

14. McKinsey, I. (2019, January 2019). Blockchain's Occam Problem. McKinsey&Company. https://www.mckinsey.com/industries/financial-services/ourinsights/Blockchains-occam-problem

15. Zavolokina, L., Ziolkowski, R. and Bauer, I., 2020. Management, Governance, and Value Creation in a Blockchain Consortium. *MIS Quarterly Executive*, 19(1), pp.1-17.https://www.researchgate.net/publication/336967927_Management_Governance_and_Value_Creation_in_a_Blockchain_Consortium

16. Which Governments Are Using Blockchain Right Now? – Consensys.net https://consensys.net/blog/enterprise-Blockchain/which-governments-are-using-Blockchain-right-now/

17. Furlonger, David. *Real Business Of Blockchain*. Harvard Business Review Press, 2019.

18. Mahankali, Srinivas, *Blockchain for Non-IT Professionals: An Example Driven, Metaphorical Approach* . Notion Review Press, 2020

19. The Role of APIs In Blockchain | Nordic APIs – https://nordicapis.com/the-role-of-apis-in-Blockchain/#:~:text=Utilizing%20the%20Blockchain%20to%20facilitate,and%20was%20in%20fact%20legitimate.

20. The Challenges of Blockchain Interoperability – PrimaFelicitas – https://www.primafelicitas.com/the-challenges-of-Blockchain-interoperability/#:~:text=Challenges%20for%20Blockchain%20Interoperability&text=The%20most%20major%20challenge%20to,several%20standardization%20efforts%20in%20progress.

21. Top 7 Ways to Make Your Blockchain Consortiums Work – https://www.kaleido.io/Blockchain-blog/top-7-ways-to-make-your-Blockchain-consortiums-work

22. McCurdy, Denise, "The Role of Collaborative Governance in Blockchain-Enabled Supply Chains: A Proposed Framework." Thesis, Georgia State University, 2020. https://scholarworks.gsu.edu/bus_admin_diss/131

23. Deloitte Global Blockchain Survey 2020 – https://www2.deloitte.com/content/dam/insights/us/articles/6608_2020-global-Blockchain-survey/DI_CIR%202020%20global%20Blockchain%20survey.pdf

24. EU Blockchain Observatory & Forum – Governance and new organizational challenges – https://www.euBlockchainforum. eu/sites/default/files/reports/workshop_9_report_-_governance. pdf?width=1024&height=800&iframe=true

25. Various Consortium Logos used in the book belong to the respective consortiums.

26. Consortiums details taken from the individual website of each consortium.

27. Innovation Insight for Blockchain Consortiums – Gartner Report

28. Morkunas, Vida & Paschen, Jeannette & Boon, Edward. (2019). How Blockchain technologies impact your business model. Business Horizons. 10.1016/j.bushor.2019.01.009.

29. Osterwalder, Alexander, and Yves Pigneur. *Business Model Generation*. Wiley, 2013.

30. Business Model Canvas – https://en.wikipedia.org/wiki/Business_ Model_Canvas

31. Do Blockchains and Consortiums go together ? – https://medium. com/@SusanJoseph1786/do-Blockchains-and-consortiums-go-together-like-pb-j-c70879c0601

32. Project Ubin Phase 5 report – Enabling Broad Ecosystem opportunities – Temasek & MAS

33. Monetary Authority of Singapore – Project Ubin https://www. mas.gov.sg/schemes-and-initiatives/project-ubin

34. Blockchain Case Study for Banking in Singapore https://consensys. net/blockchain-use-cases/finance/project-ubin/

35. World Economic Forum -Blockchain Interoperability https:// www.weforum.org/whitepapers/inclusive-deployment-

of-blockchain-for-supply-chains-part-6-a-framework-for-blockchain-interoperability

36. Towards Blockchain 3.0 Interoperability: Business and Technical Considerations – University of Arkansas BC CoE 2019-01O – Zach Steelman, Mary Lacity, Paul Cronan . https://cpb-us-e1.wpmucdn.com/wordpressua.uark.edu/dist/5/444/files/2019/05/BCCoEWhitePaper012019Open.pdf

37. Itransition Interoperability Explained – https://www.itransition.com/blog/blockchain-interoperability

38. ETorox – https://etorox.com/news/opinions/the-importance-of-interoperability-for-blockchains

Glossary of Important Questions

Chapter 1: Blockchain – The world of decentralization

1. What is Bitcoin and how does Bitcoin work?

2. What is Blockchain?

3. What are the key benefits of Blockchain?

4. What are the different components of Blockchain?

5. What is meant by Consensus?

6. What are Smart Contracts?

7. How is Blockchain evolving?

8. How will you decide if Blockchain is needed for a project?

9. What is the Value Proposition of Blockchain across industries?

10. Which are the top countries exploring/leveraging Blockchain?

11. What are the potential applications of Blockchain in Smart Cities?

Chapter 2: Blockchain Consortium

1. What is a Consortium?

2. What is Blockchain Consortium?

3. Why Consortiums are critical for Blockchain Technology?

4. What are the benefits of Blockchain Consortium?

5. What are all the roles a Blockchain Consortium can play?

6. Which industry verticals are exploring, or have formed Consortiums?

7. Why are Consortiums critical for Blockchain Technology?

Chapter 3: Blockchain Consortiums – Different Flavours

1. What are the different business models of Blockchain Consortiums?

2. What are the different types of Blockchain Consortiums?

3. Which are the industries ideal for forming a Consortium?

4. What are the key considerations of a Blockchain Consortium business model?

5. What are the main business models of a Consortium?

6. What are for-profit and non-profit Blockchain Consortium business models?

Chapter 4: Consortium Formation

1. What key questions should decision makers of organizations consider before determining which type of Consortium is right for them?

2. What is Pre-Consortium agreement?

3. How important is Pre-Consortium agreement?

4. What are the challenges to be addressed during Pre-Consortium agreement?

5. What are the steps of Blockchain Consortium formation?

6. Understand the formation of Blockchain Consortium with a real-life example.

7. What are the concerns to be addressed during Consortium formation?

Chapter 5: Consortium Governance

1. What is meant by Governance?

2. What is Blockchain Consortium Governance?

3. How important is the role of Governance for Blockchain Consortium?

4. What are the components of Blockchain Consortium Governance?

5. What concerns should the workgroups focus on addressing?

6. What are the different Governance Models used for Blockchain Consortium?

7. Learn about different Governance models with examples.

8. What are the different facets of Blockchain Consortium Governance?

9. What are some of the data policies a data governance should specify?

10. What are the risk factors one should understand and manage in Blockchain Consortium?

11. What are the challenges faced in Blockchain Consortium?

12. How to get started in conceptualizing a governance framework?

Chapter 6: Making business sense of Blockchain Consortium

1. How Blockchain Consortiums make business sense.

2. How to build a Business Canvas Model for Blockchain Consortium?

3. How to get started with conceptualizing a Business Model canvas for a Blockchain Consortium you are planning for?

Chapter 7: Blockchain Consortium – Readiness Assessment Tool

1. How do you assess if you are ready to join a Consortium?

2. How do you measure your readiness to join a Consortium?

3. What are the different dimensions that decision makers can use to assess their readiness?

Chapter 8: Conclusion

1. What are the desirable elements a Blockchain Consortium should comprise of?

2. What are the key learnings that would help future Blockchain Consortiums?

3. What is meant by Interoperability?

4. Why is Interoperability important for Blockchain Consortiums?

5. What is Blockchain Interoperability Model?

6. What are the different approaches to achieve Blockchain Interoperability?

7. What are the examples of Blockchain Interoperability?

8. What is the importance of AI and IoT in Blockchain Consortium?

General

1. Why should you join a Consortium?

2. What are the advantages/benefits of joining a Consortium?

3. What should you be aware of when joining a Consortium?

4. Do you want to know if your business/organization can join a Consortium?

5. Is joining Blockchain Consortium a good decision?

6. What to look for in a Consortium to join?

7. Are you planning to start a Consortium?

8. How to start a Consortium?

9. Do you want to see examples of Consortiums at different stages?

10. How do you check your preparedness to join a Consortium?

11. How does a Consortium take Blockchain technology R&D to the next level?

12. What is the current state of Blockchain Consortiums across the globe?